H.E.A.L.I.N.G.

A Guide to the Grieving Process

Jenene Holcomb

Printed in the United States of America

First Printing March 2022

ISBN 978-1-956661-08-8 Paperback

Photographs on pages 40, 53, 63, 78, 80
Betsy Hoyt Feinberg

Published by: Book Services
www.BookServices.us

Contents

Dedication

For Lee, your love surrounds me and gives me strength.
You made this possible.
I love you still.

Acknowledgements

I am filled with gratitude for the many people who provided support and contributions to this book:

For my parents, who loved me unconditionally and taught me to walk in faith. They are always my biggest cheerleaders.

For my children, Brittany and Caleb, who bring me unending joy and fill my heart with so much love. I am blessed to share this earthly journey with them.

For Ty, my amazing and loving friend, who constantly encouraged me to write this book. I am so grateful to have you in my life.

For my first readers—Bonnie, John, Galen, Britt, and Ty—your notes and words gave me the courage to publish. It takes special friends to be honest and vulnerable with each other. Thank you.

For my counselor, Victoria, who walked with me through my darkest days and helped me heal. I thank God for you!

For my editor, Betsy, who felt a connection with this project from the beginning. It was meant to be!

Introduction

You Are Not Alone

Stories of lives and loves tragically destroyed by chronic illness always made me shudder. I thanked God it wasn't me. It couldn't happen to *me*, could it? Our family was young and healthy. We had wonderful, fulfilling lives. Nothing to worry about. But suddenly, my own life became one of those tear-jerker stories. Cancer took my beloved husband from me and our young children.

My life changed forever in 2008. Lee was working away from home when he received the call: the tumor in his liver was malignant. He phoned me immediately to say he was coming home that day.

I remember exactly where I was and what I was doing. It was a bright, sunny July day. Our son was celebrating his tenth birthday with his friends at the swimming pool. There was cake, laughter, and singing. There were presents. My emotions abruptly shifted from happiness and delight to despair and worry, to the feeling that the earth under my feet was collapsing in an emotional earthquake.

We prayed for healing. Even with remission, however, we knew that life would never be the same.

It was not to be. In the fall of 2009, the cancer had spread to my husband's lungs, and the tumors in his liver were growing. The chemo cocktails weren't working. We switched medical facilities and doctors, trying anything to find the cure he so desperately needed. His body continued to fail. As his caregiver, I was by his side when he died. I will never forget the sights, sounds, and feelings of that day. Like a movie reel, I can replay the moments again and again in my mind. I know exactly what I was wearing, what I was thinking, the panic I was feeling, how my heart was racing, and the words that came out of my mouth. It was the most painful experience I have ever had, followed closely by having to tell my children that their father had died.

Everyone remembers where they were and what they were doing when the shocking news of 9/11 reached them. You yourself may have cried, burned with anger, plunged into depression, or stayed in a state of shock for days. It was a collective grieving experience. In the United States, we all witnessed that devastating act of terrorism. We could share our outrage, sadness, and shock with others.

But now your grieving experience, like my own, is personal, not collective. The gut punch you received when you experienced your loss will never be forgotten. Because each of us has a unique connection to loss, it often feels like we are the only one burdened by it. We often feel alone in our grief.

I want to walk with you through the grieving process to let you know you are not alone. People said to me, "You're so strong." Friends said, "I don't know how you do it." I did it; I am still doing it, thanks to the help I found along the way. In sharing my turbulent journey along the path of grief with you, I pray that you will find comfort in the tools I've discovered and in the tools that others shared with me. Some of these you may find useful, others you may not. There are no rules. Take what you want, and leave the rest.

Chapter One

What is Grief?

When people think of grief, they usually associate it with a deep sorrow, especially one caused by someone's death. But grief is actually a response to any profound loss. This loss may be physical, like the death of someone we cared for, but it can also be social: a divorce, separation, or estrangement. It can be occupational, like the loss of a job. It can be losing a home to fire.

Sorrow, misery, sadness, anguish, pain, distress, agony, torment, affliction, suffering, heartache, woe, desolation, despair, despondency, bereavement, lamentation, and pining are all listed as synonyms of grief. They don't even come close. Grief is grief. If you have experienced grief or are now actively grieving, you probably understand what I mean. Like Joan Didion says in in her book, *The Year of Magical Thinking*, "Grief turns out to be a place none of us know until we reach it."

Although grief is the response to any loss, this book will focus primarily on the physical loss of a loved one.

When you have had a loss, you may experience some or all of the following possible signs of grief:

- Crying and general feelings of sadness

- Oversleeping or difficulty falling asleep or staying asleep

- Questioning personal beliefs and relationships

- Changes in appetite, unexpected weight gain or loss

- Withdrawal from social activities and your usual hobbies

- Difficulty focusing on work, school, or other tasks

❧ Trouble maintaining personal relationships

❧ Intermittent feelings of sadness, sorrow, or depression

❧ Loss of motivation for routine activities, including self-care

Many of us lose our sense of security. It's like losing your footing before a fall. Suddenly the world is upside down and nothing makes sense. You are plunged into grief, an unimaginable landscape that is unfamiliar to you. Your world has irrevocably changed. One of the best posts I've seen on grief was on the website whatsyourgrief.com. It said it in five words, "Grief Sucks, said Everyone Ever."

The poem "For a Dear One at a Dark Time" by Alrene Gay Levine, author of *39 Ways to Open Your Heart,* touched me deeply.

For a Dear One at a Dark Time

Your world seems empty now: a puzzle with pieces
you thought made you complete, now missing.
If I could make you listen, in your loneliest hour,
the doves continue to coo and soft breezes
still strum their spring song on budding branches.

If I could help you see, in your lightless prison,
the perfection of a powder-blue-sky day
has not gone away and the courageous yellow face
of a solitary dandelion defies the gardener's rake.

If I could urge you to inhale, despite your clenched chest,
you'd be healed by the green tonic of mown grass
or even the humble aroma of a potato
baking in the oven just for you.

If I could I would teach you to taste the salt of your tears
and explore their source, to feel the jagged edges
of your newly broken heart, and with those same hands,
use the thread of your pain to sew a stronger version
whole again.

— *Arlene Gay Levine*

There is no right or wrong way to grieve, which makes writing about it difficult. Everyone's experience of the grieving process is unique and personal. You may need to grieve openly, surrounded by others. You may need to grieve privately, by yourself. Each person will require their own type of support. Yet when someone suffers a loss, they often feel alone, isolated, confused, and overwhelmed. My goal is to give comfort and offer some ideas for moving forward and ultimately healing from the pain of your loss.

It may seem obvious, but I want to remind you to take care of your physical health. Although this book is about emotional healing, that won't be possible if you are ignoring your physical needs. Bereavement can threaten your health. Right now you may not care about your health: take care of yourself anyway. Eat a balanced diet, rest, drink plenty of water, and participate in moderate exercise. Your body may be depleted both emotionally and physically, so good nourishment, breathing, and movement are important. If you are having trouble eating, you might consider a protein or dietary supplement. Avoid the abuse of drugs and alcohol. It is important to be as physically sound as you can be so that your emotional healing can begin. Do not minimize the difficulty of this step in the process. Just remember: Your life is valuable! You need to take care of it.

If you have children, don't forget them during your grieving process. They may be experiencing many of the same emotions as you, so share your thoughts and include your children when possible. This is a painful time, but they need to know that they are loved and not forgotten or dismissed. I found children's books on death and loss to be a great resource for my children. As we read them together, we discussed our thoughts and the connection each book had to our own lives.

As children mature and move through different developmental milestones, they will experience grieving in new ways. As my children grew older, I could see that they reacted to loss differently. Sometimes there was less verbal expression and more acting out behavior. I saw them withdrawn, depressed, angry, sad, overachieving, and underachieving. I tried my best to support them through their grief and let them know that their feelings were valid. It was hard since I was actively grieving too. But I realized that if I couldn't be present for them the way they needed due to my own grieving, then they needed someone else to listen to them. I could provide that. I made appointments with a local counselor for both my children and myself.

When my son, Caleb, would see me crying, he would crawl into my lap and stroke my hair. I didn't try to hide my grief from him. I think it's healthy to be honest with them and yourself. Children are not dumb. They know when something is going on. By acknowledging the difficulty of loss with them and supporting them in an age-appropriate way, you give them permission to grieve and begin healing themselves.

It seems that today everyone wants to avoid the topic of grief because our days should all be filled with rainbows and unicorns. Yet death is a part of living. When I was first thinking of writing this book, I went to Barnes and Noble to research what was available on grieving. Only a quarter of the bottom row of the self-help section was devoted to coping with grief. Above it were two and a half shelves devoted to sex! It was very illuminating to see just how uncomfortable the subject of death and grief is for our society. We would rather talk about something as intimate and personal as sex rather than death.

As much as we as a society try to ignore, discount, or reject loss, no one will be a stranger to it or to the grieving process. There are three kinds of people in this world: those who are going through a significant loss, those who have gone through a significant loss, and those who will go through a significant loss. Everybody will join our group. Grief is universal. It touches all walks of life, all races, and all peoples. It affects young and old, rich and poor. There are no barriers to grief. No one is immune to the pain of loss.

"In every person's life, some form of loss is inevitable. It might come in the form of the death of a loved one, the loss of a pet, or even the loss of a job or academic status. In each of these situations, grief is a normal response, which can take many different forms. Grief not only occurs at the death of a loved one, but may be triggered by other events. These could be the ending of relationship, such as separation or divorce, or even the loss of a feeling of safety such as a burglary or robbery of your home." *(Gradients of Grief: Understanding the Different Forms of Grief,* Kat Smith, September 12, 2019, MeMD Blog)

In Nessa Rapoport's book *A Woman's Book of Grieving,* "An Old Tale" tells the story of a grieving woman who is given a task. She is to go to every house that has not seen sorrow and beg for flour. With that flour, she is to bake a cake, and her departed loved one will be returned. The woman runs from house to house, seeking the flour. One door, then another, then another, then all in the town close to her. She is left with an empty bowl. The woman cries out that no one would help her bring her beloved lost one home. Then she feels a hand upon her head and a voice says, "My child." In that moment of compassion, she understands: "No house is immune to sorrow, and no woman from a time of solitude."

It seems to me that in today's world, we do a poor job of acknowledging grief and helping people heal from loss. In the 19th and early 20th centuries, those grieving often wore a black band on their upper sleeve, sometimes for months. Widows dressed in black for a full year. Others saw the black attire and immediately realized they were in the presence of a grieving person. You didn't need to explain why you seemed out of it or not yourself. Imagine how our society would respond today. Would we be more patient and kinder to people wearing a visual clue to the pain they were experiencing?

A mourner is anyone who has had a parent, child, sibling, or partner die. In many non-Western cultures, there is no stigma attached to the grieving person. In fact, in some of these cultures a mourner is considered legally insane for a year. These mourners are allowed to break vows, wake people in the middle of the night, change their minds and express emotions, even strong ones such as anger at the person who died. Tracey Wallace explains in "Death Rituals, Ceremonies, and Traditions Around the World" (https://eterneva.com/blog/death-rituals/) that our Western culture, including the United States, Canada, and parts of Europe, has transformed the grieving process into a self-help improvement plan. Our can-do western spirit transfers into a we-can-do-better proposition of improving ourselves through grief. This is extremely isolating and defeating. Today we are not allowed to grieve for too long. In the 1800s and early 1900s, etiquette prevented this rush to be done with mourning. Confucius said, "Let mourning stop when one's grief is fully expressed." Our current culture does not give this kind of grace or leniency to mourners. But you can offer yourself a break.

There are many of the walking wounded among us. They look fine on the outside, but emotionally they are devastated. We don't know what another person is going through. That is why it is important to practice kindness, to be gracious and compassionate when interacting with others, since we really don't know what another person is facing in their life. I was one of the walking wounded. If I could have worn a black band to display my grief, maybe people would have understood why I wasn't smiling or happy. It would have taken some pressure off of pretending to be okay. No one would have to ask, "What's wrong?" It would be evident.

Elizabeth Kubler-Ross also surmised that grief needs to be completely experienced for healing, that the only means of recovering from loss is wading through it. You can put it off, but it can't be skipped. I agree with her. I believe that trying to skip the grief or push it away will have a boomerang effect. It will come back and bite you. Much like Alice in Wonderland, the only way out is through!

What is Death?

What is death?
Death is nothing at all.
I have only slipped away into the next room.
And I am I. And you are you.
Whatever we were to each other then, that we are still.

Speak to me in the easy way that you always used to do.
Laugh as we always laughed, at the little jokes we enjoyed together.
Let my name be ever the household word that it always was.
Life means all that it ever meant.
Remember there's an absolute unbroken continuity.

Why should I be out of mind because I am out of sight?
I am waiting for you.
Somewhere very near.
Just around the corner.
All is well.

Author unknown

My background is Christian, so I will refer to God and use "He" when referring to the Creative Force/Higher Power I believe in. I do not mean to offend anyone with my beliefs. To make this more compatible with your belief system, feel free to substitute another word for "God" based on whichever representation of your faith you choose. I also take comfort in my belief that our soul is eternal and will return to the Divine or to a different plane than our earthly one. I am not alone in this belief. In fact, all of the world's major religions teach that the human soul continues after the death of the physical body. David Searls explains the eternal nature of our souls this way: "Seeing death as the end of life is like seeing the horizon as the end of the ocean." Following are some examples of the major world religions' teachings on the soul's continuation.

Hinduism:
 "Anyone who…quits his body remembering Me, will be united with me.
  Be certain of that."
Bagavad-Gita 8:5

Judaism:
 "The dust returneth to the earth as it was and the spirit shall return unto
  God who gave it."
Ecclesiastes 12:7

Buddhism:
 "That individual in this world who…is learned and virtuous here in this
  brief life; after the dissolution of the body, goeth to heaven."
Ita Vuttaka 71

Zoroastrianism:
 "The wise Lord with dominion and piety shall give us welfare
  and immortality."
Yasna 47:1

Christianity:
 "If the earthly house in which we dwell be destroyed, we have a building of
  God, a house not made by human hands, eternal in the heavens."
2 Corinthians 5:1

Islam:
 "They who believe and fear God, for them are good tidings in this life and
  in the next."
Koran 10:63, 64

Baha'i:
 "We are God's, and unto Him shall we return."
Writings of Baha'u'llah (Kitab-i-Igan, 252)

A Baha'i allegory on the possibility of eternal life after death compares the death of our physical body to a caged bird. To imagine the death of the spirit is like imagining that a bird in a cage will be destroyed if the cage is broken. The bird does not need to fear the destruction of its cage. Our physical body is like the cage and our spirit, or soul, is like the bird. Once the bird is freed from its cage, it will have greater freedom, greater perception, and greater happiness.

This brief perspective on immortality is included to give comfort to those who may be wondering what happens after death. My belief in an eternal soul will be evident in my writing. One of the greatest mysteries of life continues to be what happens after the physical body expires.

Chapter Two

Personal Perspectives

My Backstory

Before my mother's death in 2004, the loss of beloved pets, my grandparents, and a job had caused me sorrow and pain, but these losses didn't hit me as hard as my mother's. She was my best friend. Her unexpected death of a heart attack at only sixty-one devastated me. I knew I needed help, and I found a counselor who specialized in grief. These events set me on a journey to read, watch, listen, and discover more about the grieving process.

After several months of counseling, meditation and prayer, journaling and seeking, I began to accept my mother's death and feel better again. Then, only four years later, in 2008, my husband was diagnosed with cancer. He battled the agressive disease for a little over a year and died on November 4, 2009. A whole new awareness of the process of grief was given to me.

This is my personal story of my hard-won knowledge of the grieving process. I have read articles and books, watched movies and programs, participated in classes, and talked with numerous surviving loved ones, as well as counselors and clergy, about loss and living through the loss. I went through the darkest period of my life following my husband's death, yet I am still here. You, too, are still here, despite your loss. As you create your own narrative about loss and living through it, I hope my story can help you.

The Beginning of Lee's Story

I always dreamed of meeting my future husband at church, so I hate to admit this, but I met Lee at a bar called The Bank Shot in Alamosa, Colorado. The place has rows of pool tables, cue sticks on the walls, and pitchers of cold draft beer on tap. My girlfriend and I went to the Bank Shot on the Friday of Memorial Day weekend in 1993. I wasn't going to go out that night, but my girlfriend insisted. Call it fate or divine intervention or our sacred contract, but there he was, sitting on the tier above us at a table. As we were leaving, Lee walked me out to the car. He finally asked for my number, and we started dating. It was a whirlwind courtship. We were married in November of that same year.

Fast forward ten years, and we had two children, a daughter named Brittany and a son named Caleb. We had moved several times, but in 2008 we were settled on five acres of land in La Garita, Colorado. We were in a nice double-wide trailer, although I prefer the term "modular." It just sounds better, doesn't it? I was teaching preschool twenty miles away. Lee and a partner had started their own company, Rio Grande Powerline Construction. Although a challenge at first, their business was taking off. We were comfortable financially. The kids were growing up healthy and happy. Life was good.

In the spring of 2008, Lee started experiencing discomfort in his stomach. He was tested for an ulcer twice, but the tests did not show anything. He was treated for acid reflux. That helped a little, but still the pain persisted. He consulted several doctors. He specifically asked one of the doctors about cancer. She said, "No. Cancer is a silent killer. There isn't pain associated with it." She felt there was nothing to worry about. The pain didn't stop, and Lee was vomiting several times a day for weeks. Finally, a Physician's Assistant ordered a CT scan. The results came. There was a mass in Lee's liver. The scan showed several tumors, the largest about the size of a potato.

There was a biopsy and the agonizing wait for the results. I prayed for a curable and reversible liver disease, such as fatty liver disease. But no, on July 8, 2008, Caleb's tenth birthday, Lee got the results. The tumors were malignant. A voice in my head screamed, "No, no, no!" It felt like all the air in the room had been sucked away. It's hard to know how to react when such a devastating sucker punch hits you in the gut. We were scared and our future was uncertain.

We made appointments at MD Anderson in Houston, one of the best cancer treatment facilities in the United States. First, however, Lee needed a colonoscopy. We were able to get one quickly in Albuquerque, New Mexico. We began keeping a medical journal because all the appointments in Houston, Pueblo, and Denver were overwhelming. Plus, all the different medications had to be remembered.

I learned more about cancer and treatments than I ever wished to know. We tried a raw food diet, then a macrobiotic diet. We read everything we could get our hands on. We were given contradictory advice. We tried to maintain a routine day-to-day existence for the children and ourselves, but nothing was normal anymore.

It was exhausting, overwhelming, stressful, frightening, and frustrating. We tried to be positive and remain hopeful. Lee followed every medical recommendation. He suffered through chemotherapy. He lost his hair. He said he missed his nose hair the most because now there was nothing, no barrier, to stop the snot from dripping. He had swelling, nausea, and pain. Intense pain. Yet he didn't complain much. He took it all, with all the side-effects, like the strong man he was.

Somewhere in all of this, I decided that cancer wouldn't defeat me. I decided to let this experience "bring it." I would survive with myself intact—changed, of course, maybe scarred is the word, but still *me*.

After Lee's death, I changed my mind about merely surviving. That wasn't enough. I went from surviving to thriving. I remember driving home one night about sunset. The sky was a brilliant pink and orange above our gorgeous, snow-capped Mt. Blanca. I thought about all of the beauty still in this world. I wanted to see more places and experience more joy. I decided to become *more*–more passionate about my hobbies, my desires. I reinvented myself. This worked for me.

The End of Lee's Story

> *"Our way is not soft grass,*
>   *it's a mountain path with lots of rocks.*
>   *But it goes upwards, forward,*
>   *toward the sun."*
> —Ruth Westheimer

Lee and I had discussed what we wanted done with our remains upon our demise. We both knew we wanted to be cremated and have our ashes scattered in the mountains or in a river. Lee died in November, and snow had already fallen on the tallest mountain peaks surrounding our home in Colorado. My in-laws kept telling me that it would be impossible to get up Mt. Blanca due to the three-to-five feet of snow already accumulated up there. But I knew that Mt. Blanca, the beautiful, majestic mountain that dominates our valley, was where we needed to distribute Lee's ashes. It is part of the Sangre de Cristo (Blood of Christ) range in the Rocky Mountains. Mt. Blanca, over 14,000 feet above sea level, is one of the famous "fourteeners" that challenges mountaineers. It is sacred to the Navajos. The Utes called it "White Shell Mountain." It is a very special, sacred place.

It seemed that everybody was telling me I would have to wait until late spring or even summer to scatter the ashes. I emphatically did not want Lee to have to stay in a plastic container in a closet all winter. (I did not buy a fancy urn or vase because I knew we weren't going to keep the ashes.) I shared my dilemma with a couple of friends and both had the same answer: "You could fly." I had not thought of it! Fly, of course! I was relieved, excited, sad, and curious. And I wondered how on earth I was going to pull it off.

One of Lee's friends gave me the name of a mutual acquaintance who had an old U.S. Army medical helicopter from the Vietnam War. This helicopter was the kind you see at the beginning of M*A*S*H. I contacted Earl VanTreese, the owner and pilot, and we set a date to meet at our regional airport in Alamosa. Earl was a sweetheart about it all; he never accepted any monetary compensation for his fuel or his time. It was also his last flight as a pilot. Due to medication he was being required to take, he would no longer be able to pass the physical examination for his pilot's license. Bless him!

We had to have clear skies, low wind, and good flying conditions for the flight to happen. We were blessed with all three on our scheduled day.

I saved a few of the ashes in case I wanted to scatter them with my own ashes or fill a memorial necklace, but the rest flew with us up Mt. Blanca. Brittany, Caleb, Earl, and I left early on a cold and clear late November morning. The helicopter was not very fast and had to steadily climb in altitude. We putt-putt-putted up into the air towards the sacred mountain.

The cockpit was designed to hold two people, and we had two adults and two children. We were crammed in like Cinderella's step-sisters' toes in her glass slipper. Plus, the glass was magnifying the sun's rays, especially at the high altitude. I had bundled us all in heavy winter clothes, and we were sweating.

I had envisioned landing at the very highest point of Mt. Blanca, its peak at 14,326 feet. However, a helicopter needs a flat place to land. Earl was able to find a flat spot at 12,200 ft. It was just too steep to go any higher on the mountain.

The breeze was stirring slightly as we exited the helicopter. We chose a spot and emptied the ashes on the cold, hard ground. Earl took some photos of us.

Brittany, Caleb and I cried, hugged, and said a prayer for Lee. I felt sad, of course, but also pride in accomplishing this task that so many people had said would have to be postponed. An avid outdoorsman, Lee would love this wild, rugged, pristine, and sacred place. Mt. Blanca is to the east of our valley, dominating the landscape. I look at the mountain, and I feel Lee is there, connected to me throughout every day.

This was another step toward closure for my kids and me. We were truly blessed to have all the right conditions and to find the right person to help us.

On the flight back to the airport, the cockpit was even stuffier and warmer than before. Caleb gets overheated easily, and he started feeling nauseous. As soon as we opened the door of the cockpit, he vomited. A little of the throw-up got on the doorframe of the helicopter. Earl went to clean it up while I took Caleb to the airport's restroom.

As we left the facilities, a young pilot asked me if we had enjoyed our flight. When I explained that it wasn't a recreational flight and that we had scattered my late husband's ashes, his face fell. He could not stop apologizing. I assured him that it was okay. And it really was. We were okay!

I chose to tell my in-laws after the fact. I couldn't put myself through their concerns, their telling me "no," or that it would have to wait. I was, and still am, proud of myself for finding a way to make Lee's wishes happen.

Earl Vantreese died in 2019 as I started to write this book. I hope God gave Earl his wings, because he was truly an angel to my family.

Decisions like these are difficult. Carrying out the wishes of our loved ones or our plan after our loved one's parting can be challenging. I believe God planted the seed for me to accomplish my plan. He provided the right person at the right time for me to contact. After that it all fell into place. I did need to be open and willing to listen for these ideas from others to work. Like other instances in my life, I needed to ask for help. I needed to be humble and vulnerable and realize I couldn't do this alone. I "let go and let God" guide this process. That's when it all worked out!

Chapter Three

Grief is Fluid

Spring knows that winter is part of the journey.

"Grief never ends, but it changes. It's a passage, not a place to stay. Grief is not a sign of weakness, nor the lack of faith. It is the price of love." Author Jessie Stillwater used this quotation on the cover of her book on grief, and it rings true. Elizabeth Kubler-Ross wrote that our departed loved ones may actually have it easier than we do because there is no dimension of time for them, while we who mourn are stuck in time. In our grief, that moment may seem to last forever.

I am reminded of an account of a woman who lost her young niece unexpectedly. The woman wondered if she would ever smile again. Her heart was broken, and she didn't know if it could ever be repaired. She wanted to be transported into the future, to a time when the pain would lessen. I can relate. I think we have all wished for a magic wand to whisk us away from the time when our heart was broken. We want to press a fast-forward button and escape the pain. You may feel this way right now. You wonder if you will ever laugh or find joy again? You wonder if your broken heart can be healed. Ecclesiastes 3:1-4 (NIV) gave the woman comfort. "There is a time for everything, and a season for every activity under the heavens: a time to weep and a time to laugh, a time to mourn and a time to dance." We may still feel the weight of our grief, but we do not have to stay there. We can feel trapped in sorrow with no hope, but healing can happen.

In the survival stage you are just concentrating on getting through the minutes or hours of the day. You may even feel like there is nothing left to live for and long for a release from the pain. Many bereaved people have felt this, but your sense of purpose and meaning will return. The acute, raw, throbbing pain will lessen over time. That being said, there is no time limit on grief. It doesn't just magically disappear. Maria V. Snyder wrote, "An ember still smolders inside me. Most days, I don't notice it, but out of the blue, it'll flare to life." This is why we need to make peace with our sorrow and grief. We have to find a way to live with it.

How long ago was your loss? Does it even matter? Can you still be plunged back into that place where your grief is so raw, so fresh, so excruciatingly painful that it feels like someone hit you in the gut and knocked the wind out of you? Do you feel like the couch left on the curb with the "Free" sign on it? The couch that nobody wants or will take? The shabby, worn, broken piece of junk that sits there day after day looking more and more worn and dejected? Maybe you feel like the leftovers in the back of the refrigerator, food that no one wants to eat?

But how is that couch's frame? Is it still good and strong? Can you re-cover the furniture? Are you still standing? Can you reimagine your life?

I happen to like leftovers. They still nourish our bodies, and we don't have to start a meal from scratch. Can you identify with this and agree that there is hope?

Speaking of leftovers, I debated using it as the title of this book: *Leftovers*. We are the ones left here alone on this earthly plane. In a journal entry, I wrote, "I see my wrinkles, the beginning of a sag under my chin, the gray creeping into my hair. It wasn't supposed to matter because we would grow old together. We would face aging and laugh at the irony of life. But you left me here. I am a leftover."

I also considered the title *Happy—or Not So Happy Endings*. We expect the fairy-tale ending, but life rarely provides one. As Katrina Kenison says in *The Gift of an Ordinary Day*, "Life is not a one-size-fits-all proposition. It is an exploration, sometimes treacherous and terrifying. And sometimes the only way to move forward is to let go of all our cherished ideas about the way things ought to be, so that we can begin to work with the things as they are." In *The Five Things We Cannot Change* David Richo echoes Kenison: "Everything changes and ends. Things do not always go according to plan. Life is not always fair. Pain is a part of life."

I hope that as you read this book, you feel like I am there with you, holding your hand through these difficult moments. I felt very alone at times, even though my friends and family tried to help. I will be honest with my experience and as truthful as I can be. I hope my genuineness and willingness to be vulnerable will not only resonate with you, but lead you to a place of healing.

A Pueblo Indian Prayer

Hold on to what is good,
even if it's a handful of earth.

Hold on to what you believe,
even if it's a tree that stands by itself.

Hold on to what you must do
even if it's a long way from here.

Hold on to your life,
even if it's easier to let go.

Hold on to my hand,
even if someday I'll be gone away from you.

People love to say, "Time heals all wounds." I have thought about this saying a great deal. This is what I have concluded: If grief is the wound, time can soften the rawness of the pain. But there may always be a scar, a vivid reminder of the loss that cut so deeply. Time does change our perspective and can give us distance from the painful event, but I don't think it ever completely erases the wound.

People may also try to be helpful by saying, "Keep putting one foot in front of the other," or "You've got to let it go," or "Get over it." Platitudes like "It is what it is" and "This too shall pass" are generally not very helpful. When the grief is fresh and raw, I don't know any words to comfort people. I know I didn't want to let go of Lee. Tears and crying were all I could do. It's hard. Your life just changed in ways you never imagined. Your feelings are real and powerful. It is your truth in this moment. I wish I could be there now to offer you a hug or take your hand. Your grief is significant. How you feel matters.

Here is an exchange from my journal between my father and myself. He probably meant to be helpful, but read it and see how it made me feel.

The setting: the kitchen of our house in La Garita, Colorado. My dad has been visiting, attending the kid's sporting events and trick-or-treating for Halloween. It is only a week before Lee passes. Lee is still mobile, but his body is swelling with fluids. His cognitive function is starting to be impaired by the excess bilirubin accumulating in his brain. This is the exchange between my dad and me as he prepares to leave:

Dad: Keep a stiff upper lip.

Me: (giving him a reproachful look) Dad—

Dad: (sighing) This is hard.

Me: That's better. (Meaning my dad found a better way to acknowledge the circumstances and express his concern.)

Lee wanders over and joins our hug. He sees my tears and wipes them away.

Lee: It's not that bad.

Me: (Forcing a laugh)

Then we all hugged.

In my head I thought, "It *is* that bad—and worse! It will only get worse! It will not get better. This is reality—this is truth! There is no frickin' stiff upper lip! I can't just pretend everything is okay and not show it!"

When people said things like "They are in a better place" or "It was for the best" or "God needed them more," it made me feel like shouting, "Bullshit! I need them more! This is the place Lee should be!"

I would wonder, what about my own suffering? How could this be part of God's plan? How could a loving God put us through this hell? There are no easy answers, and everyone will have to come to their own conclusions. For me, faith in a loving God gave me comfort. I believe that God does not want us to suffer, but being human means to exist where death and suffering happen. I realized that God was still with me, like the popular "Footprints in the Sand" poem. Isaiah 41:10 (NIV) says, "Do not fear, for I am with you; do not be dismayed, for I am your God. I will strengthen you and help you; I will uphold you with my righteous right hand." God actually carries us through the roughest times. He doesn't forsake us, even though it may seem that way.

Be at Peace

Be at peace,
Do not fear the changes of life
Rather look to them with full hope as they arise.

God, whose very own you are, will deliver you from out of them.
He has kept you hitherto, and He will lead you safely through all things;

And when you cannot stand it, God will bury you in His arms.

Do not be afraid of what may happen tomorrow;
The same everlasting Creator who cares for you today
Will take care of you then and every day.

God will either shield you from suffering
Or will give you unfailing strength to bear it.

Be at peace,

And put aside all anxious thoughts and imaginations.

—St. Francis de Sales (revised)

In *A Grief Observed,* C.S. Lewis said, "No one ever told me that grief felt so like fear." It can seem scary and dark and uncertain. That is why sometimes just being with the mourner in silence can make a difference. There's a story about a young boy who sees his elderly neighbor crying. The youth sits next to the old man on his front porch. He doesn't say anything, just puts his small hand on the wrinkled one. The boy's mother looks out the window and notices this scene. When the boy arrives home, the mother asks her son what he said to the neighbor. The boy replies, "Nothing, I just helped him cry."

I may even think I've been there, experiencing the same sorrow or grief as you. Only I have not. That's arrogance. Everyone's experience is unique. That's why this book may help you or it may not. I'm hoping that it does. I can only offer my experience and synthesize others' wisdom on grieving from what I have read and heard in lectures, classes, counseling sessions, and workshops. My wish for you is healing, acceptance, and hope for the future.

H.E.A.L.I.N.G.

I have organized this book around the word "HEALING." Each letter in the word represents a fundamental of the grieving process.

H – Honoring the loss

E – Expressing emotion

A – Allowing possibility

L – Listening to your needs

I – Inviting help

N – No "right way"

G – Gratitude

Chapter Four

Honoring the Loss

I have found it very therapeutic to honor the memory of my loved ones. Most of these ideas did not cost much, but were, and still are, valuable to me. Preparing a ritual, whether temporary, monthly, yearly, or whatever timeframe you choose, can be cathartic.

The anniversary of your departed loved one's birth or death may be stressful. You may need to consider a new way to celebrate or remember the date. Try to allow yourself some time and space for your emotional needs. Consider how you and your family will be most comfortable spending the day and adopt a plan that will work for you during these times.

For example, my mother's birthday was November 26th, usually right around Thanksgiving and sometimes in conjunction with Thanksgiving Day. The year that she died, I couldn't stand the thought of being at my dad's house for Thanksgiving. He agreed to do something different. We went to Taos, New Mexico and stayed at a hotel. In the restaurant, the people at the next table sang "Happy Birthday." We all teared up. In the chapter on allowing possibility, you will understand when I say that my mom definitely wanted us to know she was with us!

One of the first memorial items I had made was pendants containing a small amount of Lee's ashes for everyone in his immediate family. My children and I had pendants we wore to his memorial service. For their memorial gift, Lee's brothers got replicas of shotgun shells that they could hang on the rearview mirrors of their vehicles. Lee's sister and parents received heart pendants. I gave these gifts to his family at Christmas that year, almost two months after his death.

My counselor held an annual rock painting event at her home, which was called River House. We painted rocks that symbolized our loved ones. She set out a variety of paint colors and brushes and provided a pile of rocks from which to choose. Some people used names or initials; others used symbols or colors. Some glued small items to the rocks; and some put shells, figurines, marbles, or colored glass around their rocks.

River House sat on a hill overlooking the Rio Grande River. Winding down from the beautiful log home was a path to the water. Along this path people adopted a spot and displayed their rocks and other artifacts in remembrance of their loved ones. I found a brass elk plate that I attached to a short wood post for my late husband, Lee. He loved hunting and fishing, so I hung a fishing lure off one of the hooks on the brass plate. My children also participated in this yearly activity.

After my counselor retired, and the River House changed ownership, I moved all the rocks and mementos to my own house. I created a memorial area in the corner of my front yard near my aspen trees. The rocks honor Lee, my mom, my aunt, my grandmothers, and my father-in-law. There is a statue of a turtle for my mom and a Marine bolo hanging in the tree for Lee. There are also angel statues, because I find comfort in believing in them. A stone bench near the memorial offers a quiet place to sit and contemplate, meditate, or remember.

In addition to rocks, my counselor suggested tying ribbon to trees, fences, and sticks to honor loved ones. Planting a tree or special plant can be another act of remembrance.

The holidays can be especially hard. I was dreading my first Christmas following the loss of my husband. My counselor hosted a special gathering every year that helped me survive the holidays. She called it a Holy Days gathering. Each December she invited those who had experienced a loss to come for an afternoon of remembrance. People shared a photo, letter, poem, song, or story about their loss. We took turns lighting a tall candle to signal our turn, then we shared in this safe space. No applause, no comments as each took their turn. If people had been allowed to comment, it might have turned into an expectation of reward for sharing. Or it might have turned into a contest to out-grieve one another. At one of the gatherings, my counselor, Victoria, shared the story of the loss of her son. A woman said, "That's beautiful." Victoria had to stop and remind us all that we were to say nothing, an important point to note if you ever want to host your own gathering. Since I love music, I usually shared a song. One year I read a book titled *Old Turtle* because my mom loved turtles.

Honestly, without the opportunity to grieve during the "happiest time of the year," I don't know how I would've gotten through it. People expect you to be happy and jolly around Christmastime, but those who have recently gone through a loss may not feel very happy. Following my counselor's retirement, I decided to continue the tradition. I have held two Holy Days gatherings at my home now.

I have heard of churches holding a Blue Christmas service in which losses are honored. Our local United Methodist Church holds an All Saints Day service at the end of October every year. The intent is similar to the Holy Days gathering in which losses are honored. Here is an excerpt from the bulletin of an All Saints Day service at the First United Methodist Church in Alamosa, Colorado.

Prayer of Remembrance

(This prayer is meant to be responsive, with the "L" for the leader's part and the "C" for the congregation's response.)

L: *Ever-living God, this day revives in us memories of loved ones who are no longer with us. What happiness we shared when they walked among us! What joy, when loving and being loved, we lived our lives together!*

C: *Their memory is a blessing forever.*

L: *Months or years may have passed, and still we feel near to them. Our hearts yearn for them. Though the bitter grief may have softened, a duller pain remains, for the place where they once stood is empty now. The links of life are broken, but the links of love and longing cannot break.*

C: *Their souls are bound up in ours forever.*

L: *We see them now with eyes of memory. Their faults forgiven, their virtues grown larger. So does goodness live, and weakness fade from sight. We remember them with gratitude and we bless their names.*

C: *Their memory is a blessing forever.*

L: *And we remember as well, those people, who all but yesterday were part of our congregation and community. To all who cared for us and labored for all people, we pay tribute. May we prove worthy of carrying on the tradition of our faith, for now the task is ours.*

C: *Their souls are bound up in ours forever.*

L: *We give you thanks that they now live and reign with you. As a great crowd of witnesses, they surround us with blessings and offer their hymns of praise and thanksgiving.*

C: *They are alive forever more. Amen.*

Every year since my mom's and husband's death I send those closest to them something on the anniversary of their birth or death. I try to find something inexpensive, but meaningful. To honor my mom, I have given many turtles, trinkets, jewelry, Coca-Cola cards or notepads, journals, and even an article about bargain shopping. She loved to find a good sale! I have her "personal best" sales receipt saved, along with some other precious things of hers. For Lee, I have given a keychain shaped like a lineman's boot (his occupation), an elk ornament, fishing lures, and photos. I give anything that I feel is a fitting remembrance.

I have a small altar dedicated to my mom and Lee in my room. I have two candles and a few items that belonged to them in a glass dish. This is a sacred space I created for us. You may want to create something similar for your loved one.

To this day, I do not work on the anniversary of Lee's death. I follow the same routine I started right after his death. Wearing the t-shirt we had made with his picture on the back, I make myself hot tea and listen to Five for Fighting's CD, *The Battle for Everything*. I have my kids, Lee's mother and sister come over for dinner, and we watch the DVD we used at his service. We cry and remember. I found creating this type of sacred space and sacred time healing. You may want to adopt this idea as a way to honor your loss.

You might want to make a donation in memory of your loved one. Sometimes grief can paralyze us, and channeling our energies into positive action can create forward movement. I donated to the American Heart Association for my mother and the American Cancer Society for Lee. I also donated to a local cancer fund. Giving can express our hope for a better future and help to make changes we would like to see.

At seventeen, best-selling author Hope Edelman lost her mother to breast cancer. Overwhelmed with grief, her pain would not stop. She spent the first Mother's Day without her mother trying to pretend that none of it had happened. Realizing that this holiday can be more painful than pleasurable, Hope created her own healing ritual and invited others to join her. To honor those mothers who have passed, Hope and a group of women in New York City started a Motherless

Daughters luncheon in 1996 on Mother's Day. Since its inauguration, the event has grown to include dozens of other cities, including Vancouver, Canada and Melbourne, Australia. She and her cohost, Claire Bidwell Smith, also hold retreats. Motherless Daughters support groups have sprung up, not only across the United States, but all over the world.

Now 57, Hope continues her own grieving and healing process. Although her mother is not living, Hope says, "She's still the woman who had more influence on me than anyone else." Hope wanted to build community and offer a vehicle for others to express their grief and sorrow collectively. Like the Holy Days gathering or Blue Christmas, this annual Mother's Day luncheon honors the loss in our life.

Positive action can also be more private, perhaps a one-on-one visit with someone dear. You may sit with someone, really listen to another, or send a note, an email, or text. You can check in with others to let them know you care. When we remove judgment and are truly being there for someone without our own agenda or advice-giving, it allows for great inner space to be opened. It is not only freeing, but healing.

If you are looking for more ways to honor those who have gone before us, I highly recommend the book *Passed and Present: Keeping Memories of Loved Ones Alive* by Allison Gilbert, illustrated by Jennifer Orkin Lewis. Gilbert shares eighty-five heartfelt ideas for remembering our loved ones, including a memory quilt. Before I even read this book, I had the same idea, and I had quilts made out of Lee's t-shirts for my son and daughter. I presented the quilts to them at their high school graduations in memory of their father.

When Delia Ephron lost her sister, she felt like time should stop, that it would be the decent thing to do. Instead, she writes in her book *Sister, Mother, Husband, Dog*, "The clocks keep ticking, insulting our grief, forcing us into new realities, cheering us up, making us laugh, taunting us with the possibility of forgetting, zapping us with the pain of remembering."

Country music star Reba McEntire says it beautifully in a song: "I guess the world didn't stop for my broken heart." It is true. The world will keep spinning and others will seem to be getting on with their lives. You may feel very alone. I believe that's another reason why honoring our loved ones is so important. It creates a sacred space. It makes the world stop, at least for a short while.

Chapter Five

Expressing Emotions

"My soul is a broken field, plowed by pain."
—Sara Teasdale

As a preschool teacher, I teach social-emotional lessons daily. One of the themes is emotions and feelings. Like my preschool students, we often narrow emotions to three. It is easy to remember mad, sad, and happy. Yet there are so many more feelings, each with subtle nuances. Many theorists have argued that there are six to seven common human emotions. But the latest research identifies twenty-seven categories of emotion. Here are some of the categories with their variations as an example:

Happy: calm, cheerful, confident, content, delighted, excited, glad, loved, proud, relaxed, satisfied, silly, terrific, thankful, tickled

Sad: ashamed, awful, disappointed, discouraged, gloomy, hurt, lonely, miserable, sorry, unhappy, unloved, withdrawn, woeful

Angry: annoyed, destructive, disgusted, frustrated, fuming, furious, grumpy, irritated, mad, mean, pissed, violent

Other: afraid, anxious, bored, confused, curious, embarrassed, jealous, moody, responsible, scared, shy, uncomfortable, worried

It is important to be aware of the different kinds of feelings so that when you are upset, you can name what is happening to you. For example, disappointed is different from sad, and frustrated is different from mad. Identifying what you are feeling will help you communicate your needs more accurately and lead to greater understanding of yourself and your truth.

The more connected you can be to your emotions, the easier it will be for you to deal with life's challenges and understand your response to them. Acknowledging our emotions can help us not feel stuck in them. When we can tune in to the emotion and become aware of the feeling, it generally lessens their effect.

Elizabeth Kubler-Ross identified five stages of grief. These stages, which are denial, anger, bargaining, depression, and acceptance have become well known and popular. So popular, in fact, that there is a humorous, but accurate, meme comparing them to margarine and butter! In the meme, denial becomes "I can't believe It's not butter!" Anger is correlated with the photo, "What, not butter!" Bargaining is associated with "Could it be Butter?" Depression is tied to "Unbelievable! This is not butter." And finally, the photo for acceptance is a tub of plain old margarine.

When I experienced the death of my mom, I wrote the following in my journal. It illustrates the denial I was feeling:

At first I wanted to believe it was a joke—a really, really bad prank. Then I wanted to believe it was not true—it was all a mistake. I didn't know how I would make it through one hour, one night, or one week, without you. Now it has been three months and still my heart aches and my throat seizes up, my eyes swim with tears, yearning for you. What I miss most is someone to be honest with, that understands and loves me unconditionally, no matter what. To say you are missed is an understatement. I have to face the rest of my life without you here. Now I long for peace.

We want to take the five stages—denial, anger, bargaining, depression and acceptance—and put them into a checklist. Then we can systematically mark them off as we progress through them. But this is not how the stages work. My counselor worked at Elizabeth's ranch in Arizona. Elizabeth was adamant about these stages being very fluid and in no particular order. They are tools to help us identify the emotion we may be feeling. You may not experience every stage. You may have gone through one stage and revisit it again later. There is no order of progression. They are not linear, and there is not a timeline to "accomplish" the emotion.

Jennie Wright, author of *Back To Life: Your Personal Guidebook To Grief Recovery,* lists the following seven stages of grieving on the website www.recover-from-grief.com"

❧ Shock and denial

❧ Pain and guilt

❧ Anger and bargaining

❧ Depression

❧ Reflection and loneliness

❧ The upward turn, reconstruction, and working through

❧ Acceptance and hope

Doing the work associated with grief is not easy. I keep referring to the "grieving process" rather than "grief" because a process is defined as "a series of actions or steps taken in order to achieve a particular end." The grieving process is active, constantly changing, varied, and complex.

Did I experience these emotions? Yes! I also had anticipatory grief. When Lee first received his diagnosis of cancer, we were hopeful that treatment would cure him. After a year of treatment, it became evident that there would be no miracle for us. I mourned the decline of his health and his probable death. Anticipatory grief still did not prepare me for the overwhelming emotions I felt following the loss of Lee. Some of you will have anticipatory grief and some of you will not.

I tried to be gentle with myself and allow emotion to bubble up within me. Then I would try to let it go. I cried often. Anger fueled me. Sometimes the anger even gave me the energy to accomplish difficult tasks. I experienced bargaining with a hopeful twist to it. As in, "Lord if you help me through this, I will..." When I felt depressed, I played Spider Solitaire on the computer. Somehow it soothed me.

Our emotions are not signs of weakness. It is normal to feel scared, angry, sad, worried—the whole gamut of feelings. You may feel knocked down and have a difficult time getting through the day. This is hard!

One of the emotions I was surprised to feel after Lee's passing was relief. I had been the sole caregiver, and although I wasn't ready for him to die, the burden of caring for a terminally ill spouse was unrelentingly stressful and time-consuming. My patience was tested over and over again. Lee was very demanding and hard on me. He felt he needed to toughen me up. One time I was cleaning our pantry because of a mouse invasion. As I was wiping the shelves with a bleach solution to sanitize them, Lee talked to me from the living room. He was making a verbal list of everything I still needed to do that day. It was quite a long list. At the end of his demands he said, "What will you do without me?" In my mind I thought, "Maybe I'll be able to breathe." But I knew better than to say that or World War III would've broken out in my own home. I sank down to my knees crying and sobbed, "I don't know. I don't know." But I did know there would be freedom from the demands of caretaking. Then I felt guilty for even having these thoughts. I know I am not alone in these feelings.

Another time I was reading *The Last Lecture* by Randy Pausch. Lee asked me what I was reading, so I told him and summarized the book. The author, Pausch, was diagnosed with pancreatic cancer. He was a professor and a family man with a wife and two young children. Pausch carefully planned a last lecture, his final words and advice to his family about living. He was thoughtful and proactive, actually planning to make things easier for his wife by moving her to be closer to her family. He thought she would need support after his death. Lee looked at me after my summary and said, "Huh. I bet you wish you had married that guy. Well, that ain't happening here!"

I can't imagine Lee's pain at knowing he wouldn't see his children grow up, graduate, get married, and start families of their own. I know that the people we love the most not only get our very best, but often they receive our worst, too. Lee did not make his final days easy for me, although at times he was sweet, loving, and appreciative of all that I was doing to care for him and the kids. He was dealing with extremely stressful issues: physical pain, overwhelming feelings, and his own grief. I can offer that insight into Lee's behavior, and I know he thought he was helping me by "toughening me up." After he died, I did feel some relief from his harsh expectations of me. This feeling of relief was soon replaced by guilt.

I think guilt is an intense emotion that isn't often discussed with loss. We tend to sweep the guilt under the rug. Now that the loss has happened, people figure it does not matter anymore. I don't have any real answers for relieving guilt. I try to live every day without regrets, and that helps. I do feel guilty about a few things that happened in the relationships between myself and my mom and myself and Lee. Let me explain the situations to you.

When Lee was in the last stages of cancer, our pastor came to visit at our home. I wanted to talk to the pastor, but Lee was needing attention. Hospice had set up the hospital bed in the living room. Our home had an open floor plan, so we put Lee's bed where he could feel part of everything. I moved toward Lee and gently backed him up to bed. I asked, "Do you want to dance?" He shook his head. I kept maneuvering him, really herding him, towards the bed. At the edge of the bed he mustered all his strength and shouted, "Goddammit Jenene! Just leave me alone!" He managed to cuss in front of the pastor and put me in my place. I was mortified by his outburst. I moved away and he stood there. Sensing my torment, the pastor excused himself to leave. I left Lee alone for quite awhile. About an hour later he wanted in the bed. After that, he never left it.

I wish I had handled the situation differently, to be sure. I wish I had allowed him time to make his decision and not been so anxious to have him out of my way that day. Granted, I had no idea that he would not get out of that bed again.

I also feel guilty over a situation with my mother. My mom was an administrative assistant at a state prison in eastern Colorado. She quit her job to take care of our two young children when I went back to teaching. When she quit her job, she wanted assurance that this gig, as she called it, would last several years. I assured her it would. After only a year, Lee decided he was very unhappy with the rural electric company he was working for and began looking at other options. He received a job offer in the San Luis Valley of Colorado. We moved after only a year of Mom's baby-sitting position. My mom was able to return to the state prison system, but she had to commute an hour and a half each way at lower wages than before. She also dealt with some administrators who were extremely difficult people during that time. She finally managed to get back to the facility close to her home, but it was extremely stressful for her. She retired from that position happily at sixty-one. She died two weeks later of a heart attack. We all know that stress can be a contributing factor to heart disease. Even though my mom told me often that baby-sitting her grandkids was one of the greatest joys of her life and she didn't regret anything, I am still working to express my grief over this and reconcile with it. I know she forgives me, but it is harder to forgive myself.

Soliloquy

I never held her hand. I never called the last week of her life. I meant to make the trip and then postponed it. I said some words I never can take back.

If only I had known.
(Ah, but you didn't.)

If only I had thought.
(But you could not.)

Why didn't I invite you?
(Never mind.)

I hated you for growing weak, for dying.
(I absolve you.)

I lie awake remembering how I failed you.
(How I love you.)

For the rest of my life, I never—
(Only love.)

How could I—?
(Don't you know you are forgiven?)

If only—
(Would you want your child to live with such reproaches?)

No, I say reluctantly, I would not.
(Then forgive yourself. If only I could ask you, that is what I'd ask.)

From Nessa Rapoport: A Woman's Book of Grieving

I believe that if we bury the emotions and don't express them, it can lead to "dis-ease," illness that occurs when unresolved issues or buried emotions manifest themselves as physical symptoms. Pent up emotions can be like a volcano ready to erupt. It may be overwhelming to even begin to separate your emotions after a loss. You may be feeling many emotions simultaneously. This is why it is crucial to express them. This may be to a counselor, therapist, trusted friend, family member, a journal, or a pet. Talk to someone, write, draw, dance, or paint. Find a way that works for you. Henry Maudsley, a 19th century psychiatrist, said "The sorrow which has no vent in tears may make other organs weep."

As mentioned earlier, we all grieve differently. You may be surprised by the emotions you feel. Try to accept them. They are not right or wrong, they just are. Your feelings are real and they are valid. Acknowledge your pain and accept the ups and downs. (And it may seem like there are a lot more downs than ups).

Try not to judge yourself for your emotions, and don't worry about what others think. Each of us must find our own path through the darkness. Author Katie Kacvinsky says in a post on Goodreads, "Pain's like water. It finds a way to push through any seal. There's no way to stop it. Sometimes you have to let yourself sink inside of it before you can learn how to swim to the surface." Avoid feeling guilt or embarrassment over what you are feeling. Stay true to yourself.

You may feel like you have lost your joy. You may even feel guilty when you laugh or smile again. Someone said, "There is no happiness—there is life and making the best of it. There is heartache and pain and learning how to just live again. There is truth and facing it even though we don't want to. There is courage in being truthful and cowardice in denial."

But keeping yourself from enjoying life's moments won't bring them back. We tend to feed this irrational belief that by neglecting our needs and feeding our guilt and denying joy, we can resurrect our loved one. I believe our loved ones would want us to still lead a full life, one not bound by sorrow or regret. They want us to continue to grow and experience all of the best in our lives.

To Bless the Space Between Us

For Grief:
When you lose someone you love,
Your life becomes strange,
The ground beneath you gets fragile,
Your thoughts make your eyes unsure;
And some dead echo drags your voice down
Where words have no confidence.

Your heart has grown heavy with loss;
And though this loss has wounded others too,
No one knows what has been taken from you
When the silence of absence deepens.

Flickers of guilt kindle regret
For all that was left unsaid or undone.

There are days when you wake up happy;
Again inside the fullness of life,
Until the moment breaks
And you are thrown back
Onto the black tide of loss.

Days when you have your heart back,
You are able to function well
Until in the middle of work or encounter,
Suddenly with no warning,
You are ambushed by grief.

It becomes hard to trust yourself.
All you can depend on now is that
Sorrow will remain faithful to itself.
More than you, it knows its way
And will find the right time
To pull and pull the rope of grief
Until that coiled hill of tears
Has reduced to its last drop.

Gradually, you will learn acquaintance
With the invisible form of your departed;
And when the work of grief is done,
The wound of loss will heal
And you will have learned
To wean your eyes
From that gap in the air
And be able to enter the hearth
In your soul where your loved one
Has awaited your return
All the time.

—*John O'Donohue*

I found myself attending funerals and memorial services more often than I had in the past. I read many stories about the death of a loved one; I watched tear-jerkers. I had always cried easily before. After Lee's death I was even more sensitive. I actively found outlets where it was safe to cry: books, movies, and other services. These were socially acceptable outlets for showing emotions. This method may help you express emotion too.

> *"Sadness hides in the shadows of the stars. I look up when I walk so the tears won't fall." —Kyu Sakamoto from the song "Sukiyaki"*

Remember that even Jesus wept at the news of his friend Lazarus' death. John 11:35 is the shortest verse in the Bible, but it carries a lot of meaning: "Jesus wept."

The following is a prayer from a memorial service, with reference to Jesus' sorrow over his friend's death:

> *Jesus, You consoled Martha and Mary in their distress. Draw near to us who mourn for our loved ones. Jesus, You wept at the grave of Lazarus, your friend. Please comfort us in our sorrow. Jesus, You raised the dead to life. Give our departed loved one eternal life. Comfort us in our sorrows at the death of our loved one. Let our faith be consolation and eternal life our hope. Amen*

Crying is a healthy expression of grief that can release built-up tension for the mourner. Biochemist William Frey explains, "The only physiological mechanism we've evolved to alleviate stress that is different from every other animal is the ability to cry emotional tears." He discovered that 85% of women and 73% of men report feeling better after crying due to a stressful situation. ("Go Ahead – Cry!" *Parade* magazine, January 5, 1997). "...there was no need to be ashamed of tears, for tears bore witness that a man had the greatest of courage, the courage to suffer," said Viktor E. Frankl in *Man's Search for Meaning*.

In *On Grief and Grieving* Elizabeth Kubler-Ross and David Kessler state that while a part of your departed loved one lives on in the new you, a part of you also was lost with their death. They say that you should cry "whenever and wherever you want." Cry freely as you feel the need. Emotions need to be expressed; just do them in a healthy and acceptable way. A Native American proverb says, "The soul would have no rainbow if the eyes had no tears."

> *"It's so curious one can resist tears and behave very well in the hardest hours of grief. But then someone makes you a friendly sign behind a window, or one notices that a flower that was in bud only yesterday has suddenly blossomed, or a letter slips from a drawer...and everything collapses."*
>
> *Colette*

Anger is another common reaction to loss. Anger needs expression; just do it in a safe and acceptable manner. After the death of her father, one of my cousins said, "I'm so damned mad all the time." You may feel mad at the unfairness of the loss, the situation you now find yourself in, or family members. If your loss is due to the death of a loved one, you may find yourself angry at them! I was angry that Lee had left me on my own to deal with the completion of our house. So many decisions needed to be made! The responsibility of overseeing the construction of the new home was a huge weight on my shoulders. One time I was at a Home Depot trying to decide on light fixtures for the new home, and I just could not find anything I liked. I started crying in the middle of the lighting aisle because all I could think was that Lee should be there with me. It was supposed to be *our* house, not *my* house!

Every day people ask each other, "How are you?" to be polite. People will ask you after your loss too. Before losing Lee, I would usually say, "Good." After his loss, I didn't feel "good." So if people asked, I changed my response to either "okay" or "hanging in there." If I knew the person well, I might respond with "It's hard, but I'm here."

I think people don't realize how difficult it can be to answer that question. How do you be honest without alienating others or making the conversation uncomfortable? My way was to downgrade my response. It seemed important to me to speak my truth. It still is important to me. It took me a long time to answer "good" to "how are you?" But one day the answer came out "good," and it surprised me. Then I thought about it and decided I *was* "good." It was different than before the loss of Lee, but I was healthy and on the path to healing. I was "good." My life was filled with blessings, and I was grateful for them. I am grateful to have been married to Lee even though I wanted more years with him. We were blessed with two beautiful children together, and we built our early lives together. I remember these things and I tell that to Lee silently every day.

Sometimes I felt crazy. I felt like I was losing my mind. I look at this time like a big pendulum pushed the furthest from the center that it could go. But the pendulum will gradually swing back to stability. That force, that momentum won't last forever, like the law of attraction. Life will eventually return to a more balanced state.

Chapter Six

Allow Possibility

After Lee's death, I invited—no, more than that—I actively sought activities to challenge myself. I climbed Mt. Blanca, the mountain that is practically in my back yard. At 14,351 feet, its summit is the fourth highest in the Rocky Mountains. I entered a local tennis tournament and won in my division! I felt bold and empowered in a way, because I knew I could survive whatever life handed me. I opened myself to possibilities. I got a memorial tattoo. And believe me, I am not a tattoo type of girl. I was really nervous. But I love it. It is a heart-a-fly, like a butterfly, but with a heart-shaped body. In the middle is the name "Lee." Lee was my late husband's nickname and also my late mother's maiden name, so it is in memory of both of them. It is permanently perched on my right side a little below my waist. It only shows when I want it to show, like when I wear a bikini. It is big and full of bright colors—turquoise, orange, scarlet—with black lettering. Even the pain of getting it made me remember I was alive. The butterfly symbol is also significant to me. It symbolizes rebirth and hope.

It's amazing what you can do when you're already half-crazy from grief, making a statement about love, honoring your loved one's memory, and proving to yourself you can do the unexpected with boldness and courage. No matter my future relationships, this tattoo is a tangible, vivid reminder of the one I loved first and a testament to the courage to embrace change. "Just when the caterpillar thought the world was over, she became a butterfly."

In her book *A Letter to a Child With Cancer* Elizabeth Kubler-Ross says, "When we have done all the work we were sent to earth to do—we are allowed to shed our body, which imprisons our soul like a cocoon [sic] encloses the future butterfly... and when the time is right, we can let go of it and we will be free of pain, free of fears, and worries—free as a very beautiful butterfly, returning home to God, which is a place where we are never alone—where we continue to grow and to sing and dance, where we are with those we loved (who shed their cocoons earlier) and where we are surrounded with more love than you can ever imagine!"

Many people challenge themselves to go beyond their comfort zone following a personal loss. I read an article about a widow who had always wanted to go on a cruise. She didn't go on that trip with her husband as they had planned, but she arranged a trip with friends and had a magnificent time. Her next goal was to go skydiving!

Another article featured a widow who missed her husband's jokes terribly. They had been married for many years, and everyone looked to him for a laugh to brighten their day. He sounded like a character. She tentatively memorized some jokes and started telling them to friends. Soon she became more comfortable telling amusing stories and jokes and found she enjoyed the laughter of others. Her husband had always been the life of the party, but now she was developing her own talent. People started saying, "You're so funny!"

A widowed friend of mine in her late fifties trained and competed in a half triathlon. She set goals, trained hard, and reached them. Since I am younger than she is, I told her, "This sounds weird, but I'm proud of you!" With tears in her eyes, she smiled and said, "Thank you."

The next story comes from Wisconsin. A widow saw a bird that was unusual in her area soon after the death of her husband. She has seen the same woodpecker during the past five years. She feels it is her husband appearing at her weakest moments.

Can a bird be a messenger from our loved ones on the other side? Another friend of ours told his grandchildren before he passed that they could always find a feather. Can a feather be a gift from a loved one on the other side?

One time I was driving, and a beautiful buck stopped me in the middle of the road. He stayed for several seconds. I felt it was a message from Lee. Also, after Lee's death I saw more shooting stars than I had ever seen before. Coincidence? I don't think so. I believe that the soul is eternal. Our physical bodies are just a shell for the soul. When Lee died, this was so evident. He was no longer with us. I believe our loved one's souls do go to another plane. Some would call it Heaven. Our departed loved ones may try to tell us that they are okay or that they still love us. Allow the possibility!

After You Lose Someone You Love by Allie and Dave Dennison is written in diary form by three young children whose father dies unexpectedly. In Amy's entry, written twenty-two months after her father's death, she writes, "If we ever see a rainbow...I believe it's a sign from Dad telling us that we're doing great. There are other signs, too—like certain songs on the radio, a black Z-28 Camaro like Dad drove, and other things like that."

On the drive to my mother's memorial service, a huge, vivid rainbow appeared in the valley on La Veta pass in the Sangre de Cristo mountains. It lasted at least twenty minutes, which is rare in Colorado. I believe my mom was sending us a message that she was still with us, and that she was doing okay.

My mom loved to shop, especially for items on sale. How she loved a great bargain! One week following her death, I had to go shopping for a flower girl dress for my daughter. As I entered several stores in the Citadel Mall in Colorado Springs, the second largest city in Colorado, I kept seeing the same sixtyish woman. While we were both waiting near a dressing room, she said, "I am so jazzed. It's my birthday, and I am here shopping with my daughter!" I politely said how great that was, even though I was dying inside at the thought of never getting to shop with my mom again. When we entered the restaurant across the street from the mall, there was the same woman! She said, "Well, here you are again! I just feel like I need to give you a hug!" And she did. There is no doubt in my mind that my mom guided that woman to hug me. Thanks, Mom!

Music may be another way our loved ones communicate with us. After attending the service for a former student of mine who died tragically in a one-car accident, the song "Can You Feel the Love Tonight" from the Lion King came on the radio. One of this young man's former classmates had just told the story of his singing this very song during a math class when everyone was frustrated by the problems they needed to solve. I don't think it was a coincidence.

Sister Dang Nghiem, in the article "The Healer" (*Prevention,* January 2014) had another idea on allowing possibility. She says, "You can learn to call on the spirit of that person for help and learn to see him or her around you. When I see a purple flower, I remember that John (her deceased partner) loved purple flowers, and I smile. That flower, in that moment, becomes him."

Every time I see a butterfly or a turtle I am reminded of my mother. My mother owned a large collection of turtles, and many of them are displayed in my home. Winnie-the-Pooh and Piglet's conversation illustrates why I so dearly love the imagery of butterflies:

"How does one become butterfly?" Pooh asked pensively.

"You must want to fly so much that you are willing to give up being a caterpillar," Piglet replied.

"You mean to die?" asked Pooh.

"Yes and no," he answered. "What looks like you will die, but what's really you will live on."

Contemporary writer and poet Rupi Kaur explains, "You do not just wake up and become the butterfly. Growth is a process."

Chapter Seven

Listen to Your Needs

The morning of the day Lee died, I decided to clean our hardwood floors. Lee had been up the day before pacing throughout the house. His feet were swollen and weeping clear fluid, a result of the cancer. He jokingly called his feet "Shrek feet" after the ogre in the movie because of their large size. We had to cut the socks to even get them on his feet. In spite of the socks, the fluid would soak through. His footprints were all over the house. I got my floor cleaner out and went to work while Lee was asleep in his hospital bed in the living room. His sister, Debbie, had spent the night and decided to take a shower. The kids were at school. While my sister-in-law was in the bathroom, I felt an urge to spend some time alone with Lee. I stopped cleaning and put on the soundtrack to *Sleepless in Seattle*. The movie was special to us because when we first saw it, we had just announced our engagement. The movie really touched me and by the end of it, tears were streaming down my face. I cried so hard I made Lee duck through the back exit to avoid being seen by anyone. I was emotional anyway, and my breakdown was nerves and stress and maybe a premonition of how hard my love for him would be.

My inner voice told me to stop cleaning and put on the CD. I crawled into the hospital bed with Lee, held his hand, and sang along with "I Could Write a Book." Lee died that afternoon, and I will always treasure those blessed minutes with him. If I had not listened to my needs, I would have missed those precious moments with my husband while he was still alive. Please, please, listen to your inner voice!

Soon after Lee's death, my son, Caleb, wanted to join the Pee Wee Wrestling team. Caleb had tried wrestling several years before and hadn't liked it. He would usually get pinned in the first period of the match. He didn't seem too concerned about that, but he also didn't seem to be trying at all. His heart just wasn't in it. So when he asked to try wrestling again, I was surprised. Of course this was an investment of time and energy on my part. I had to get him to practice, which was 20 miles away, take him to matches, which were anywhere from 20 to 100 miles away, and help with the annual tournament, an all-day event. I asked him to be sure he wanted to do this. Yep, he was certain! I signed him up. He did the same thing as the last time, losing in the first period every match of every tournament in every town. He did place third—and got a medal!—in one tournament by getting a bye—his opponent didn't show—and then losing the final match of the day.

It occurred to me somewhere in the middle of the season that his participation had nothing to do with the sport of wrestling. It also had nothing do to with winning or losing a match. It was about so much more. His desire to join the team had to do with being around a lot of male energy, which was absent from our house now. He needed father figures—the coaches—and he needed his friends. It was never about wrestling. I am so thankful I agreed to let him participate. Caleb needed this. He listened to his needs.

My sister-in-law, Debbie, bought a miniature rat terrier a few months after Lee's death. She named the dog "Leigha," after Lee. Debbie needed more than an empty home waiting for her at the end of the day. She needed companionship. I had a German Shepherd at the time, and just seeing her wagging tail when I drove up the driveway was a joyful sight. I understood completely. My sister-in-law then adopted a rescue dog to keep Leigha company. They are her "girls," and she is completely devoted to them. They brought her comfort, and their antics made her laugh. Adopting those dogs helped her heal. She listened to her needs.

In *Dark Nights of the Soul,* Thomas Moore encourages the grieving: "Place yourself in the presence of something beautiful. It may be nature, art, culture, or family…trust that beauty can sustain you and even heal you." Where would that place be for you? Open yourself to the beauty around you and see if it benefits you.

Recording your thoughts in a journal can be beneficial. I wrote in a journal daily following Lee's death. Writing can help express your feelings and, as you look back over time, you may see progress in your healing. A journal can let us vent powerful emotions or discharge tension safely. Giving us new insights or awareness, writing can bring clarity and new meaning to significant events. Harold S. Kusher, author of *When Bad Things Happen to Good People,* writes in the foreword, "I regularly suggest to people who have suffered a particularly grievous loss to keep a written or tape-recorded journal. This helps them sort out their feelings and put them into words. It gives them a starting point from which to measure recovery."

When you go from thinking something to actually writing it down, a shift occurs. You are making a commitment to your own conscious unfolding. It is like peeling the layers off to get to the essence of the truth. William Wordsworth said, "Fill your paper with the breathings of your heart."

Writing can also make us more discriminating about the importance of things. It sharpens our focus. Only the most important things will get written, which makes you concentrate on what you value most. Finally, writing our ideas on paper can free us to make room for new avenues of thinking since we are no longer preoccupied with thoughts of losing them.

In addition to journaling or keeping a dairy, you may write letters. You may choose to write a letter to the person who died to express your thoughts and feelings. Some topics may include the following:

ᔇ A special memory

ᔇ What you miss about the relationship

ᔇ What was left unsaid, what is difficult

ᔇ Ways they will live on in you

ᔇ A question you would have liked to ask them

You may wish to write a letter to your future self, maybe one year from now. Really picture how you want to be then. Do you see yourself achieving a long-desired goal? Vacation? Purchase? Do you feel more like *you* again? Are you smiling without it feeling forced? Are you finding enjoyment in life? Do you feel at peace? Explore some possibilities. Make a list of what steps are necessary to be that person. Focus on it. Work on it. Take time for yourself to further your goals. Feel pride in each accomplishment. Along the way you may find your grief ebbing little by little as you create the you that you want to be. Am I asking you to forget? No! Some days will be extremely difficult. But try giving yourself a gift of a refined you. We have been through the fire like a fine piece of pottery. The glaze on an unfired piece of clay looks very different before going into the kiln. Surviving the fire makes the glaze shine and glisten. How do you want to come out of the other side of the fire, the grieving process? How do you really want to be?

Give yourself permission to scale back. Simply cut back on what you do. Try less: fewer emails, less texting, less social media, fewer activities. Allow yourself some space from your usual busyness.

If it is around the holidays, and it seems particularly overwhelming, give yourself permission to cut back this year. Try fewer decorations, fewer greeting cards, and less pressure to follow the traditional holiday practices. If you usually bake cookies for the holidays, and you can't wrap your head around doing it this year, by all means don't! Let someone else bake them or go without. You can also skip the holidays entirely. Acknowledge that everything is different. Accept it and plan something different or opt out. This is not about everyone else and their expectations. Do what you feel is right for you. This is *your* loss, so please, listen to your needs!

Grieving Time, a Time for Love

If a loved one has departed,
And left an empty space,
Seek the inner stillness,
Set a slower pace.

Take time to remember
Allow yourself to cry,
Acknowledge your emotions,
Let sadness pass on by.

Then center in the oneness,
Remember...God is here,
Death is but a change in form,
Your loved one is still near.

Treat yourself with kindness,
Allow yourself to feel,
God will do the mending,
And time will help you heal.

—Attributed to Barbara Bergen

Your group of friends may need to change. People may feel uncomfortable or embarrassed to be around you. Not everyone can tolerate seeing you in pain. It may be easier to talk to others who have been through a similar experience. Sharing with others who are grieving can ease loneliness. You may be feeling isolated. It may help you to be able to express your grief in an understanding environment. A grieving support group will give you an atmosphere of acceptance and under-standing. Not everyone will be able to handle your grief. Sometimes you will need to be prudent regarding who is allowed to see your vulnerability. I call them safe people, ones who can handle the emotions of the grieving process.

You may need to find a bereavement group for sharing and telling your story. Grief Share (www.griefshare.org), local churches, hospice organizations, or your mortuary may have more information or knowledge of these bereavement groups. Talkspace (talkspace.com) is a website and app that connects you to a licensed therapist.

Sharing with others who are further along in their healing process may give you hope that sometime in the future your own grief won't be so raw and painful.

If you have friends who can accept your pain through the bereavement process, talk and act naturally. You don't have to avoid the subject of your loss, making it the elephant in the room. Although conversations may seem awkward or uneasy, it is okay. I would even say it is beneficial to have these difficult conversations, if your friends are willing to walk with you through this dark time.

You may need to be by yourself for a while. When Jesus was close to finishing his earthly ministry, He went away by himself to pray without his disciples. (Matthew 14:23) The events leading up to this point in his life were both physically and emotionally overwhelming. Jesus needed time by himself to meditate and pray, in order to be reenergized to do his work. You may need to do the same.

I did go back to work only two weeks following Lee's death, but that was for Caleb, my son. He told me that he worried about my being alone at home and felt better when I was at school. Apparently, both of my children thought I was going to turn into a raging alcoholic. It wasn't easy, though. I would have to go into the bathroom at every break and every recess during the schoolday and cry. Thank goodness for waterproof mascara! Focusing on others' needs besides my own and the routine of school was good for me. Getting back into the routine of daily living may help you as well.

Although I returned to work sooner than I had planned for Caleb, I did try to be good to myself. I took naps. I refused phone calls if I didn't have the energy to talk to others. I exercised. I made myself eat. Listen to what your mind and body needs. Follow your instincts. Listen to that voice inside you. Follow what connects you to things you love and that will heal you. Remember to breathe. Move every day, even if it's just a walk to your mailbox or a jog around the block. Meditate or pray. Be good to yourself. Listen to your needs.

Chapter Eight

Invite Help

After Lee died, I remember reading about the top 10 stressful events in life. I had three out of the top five in a span of less than a year. I had the chronic illness of a loved one, the death of a spouse, and a household relocation! I was suddenly a single parent. I needed help.

When you realize you cannot do everything yourself, there will be many caring individuals waiting to be asked. They may feel uncomfortable until you ask them, so don't hesitate. Most people want to help but they don't know how or what you need. This is not the time to be proud or stubborn. This is the time to be humble and gracious. I like to be self-sufficient and not ask for help too. But it is okay to be vulnerable. Be honest with yourself and your limitations during this time. Ask yourself if you need support. There is strength in what may be perceived as weakness.

Do not worry that you are imposing on others. A caring relationship is a two-way street. Just as you are willing to help others, they are also willing to help you. We have to be open to receiving their support. We can turn to others close to us. All we have to do is ask. Please do not deny them the opportunity to help. Others have been there, and they will help share the load. There's a Swedish proverb: "Shared joy is double joy; shared sorrow is half a sorrow."

Join a support group or find a counselor or therapist. Connect with others who have similar experiences. Make no apologies for seeking help. After a huge life-changing event, why would we expect our world to be the same when it has just been turned upside down? Why would we expect ourselves to be the same and act the same? Everything changed with our loss. You changed. You are not the same person you once were.

Think about how you learned to ride a bike. You didn't just jump on a two-wheeler when you were a child and start pedaling. You learned on a tricycle or with training wheels. When you figured out how to balance and could pedal, your parents took off the training wheels, but still pushed you or ran beside you. After practicing with their support, you were finally ready to ride the bicycle independently. But you had to keep your head up and look forward: looking down meant crashing! The grieving process is like learning to ride a bicycle. You may need support through the process until you are ready to process things on your own.

After the death of your loved one, decisions need to be made about the body, a service, and what type of service. Dates need to be set. Death certificates need to be filed. Monetary arrangements need to be made. Insurance companies, government bodies, and other entities need to be notified, an obituary needs to be written. These tasks can seem overwhelming. If there is someone who can help you, let them! An elderly widow from my dad's church told me, "Don't make any big, important decisions for one year."

You may need to postpone decisions. A loss like this can leave your brain feeling fuzzy. You may not be thinking quite clearly. In the weeks following Lee's death, I felt like I was in a fog. My brain was not in peak functioning mode. Here's an example: I purchased a large canister vacuum soon after moving into our new home. A door-to-door salesman had arrived and after talking to him, I discovered we had roots in the same small hometown. This canister vacuum was quite expensive, but I traded Lee's large weight set to offset the cost. My home had mostly laminate wood floors that the vacuum was useless on. I hardly ever used the vacuum. Clearly, I had not made a wise decision.

Please monitor your rationale as best you can. Talk to someone you trust before making major life changes or purchasing high-ticket items. Learn from my vacuum mistake!

There is no timeframe for decisions on your loved one's belongings. If you want to go through their things right away and make donations or give to family or friends, that is your choice. But don't feel the need to make hasty decisions about your loved. Do not let others take over or rush you. You can make those decisions in the timeframe comfortable for you, little by little whenever you feel ready. You may need to invite help. It can seem a daunting task. Listen to your needs.

Only four months following Lee's death, my children and I moved into a new house. Lee and I had a contractor build our dream home about forty miles from our old home. It sits on 80 acres of land with stunning views of Mt. Blanca and the Sangre de Cristo and San Juan mountains. Lee got to see the house framed, but died before it was completed. I call this house his final gift to me, because with the sale of our old house and the compensation from his life insurance policy, I was able to pay off the mortgage completely.

Moving is a huge undertaking. It is stressful and hard work. Yet I found myself moving an entire household just months after my husband's death. On a muddy spring day in March we moved. I had many offers of help from Lee's friends and coworkers and I welcomed them. I had horse trailers, dollies, and muscle! There was no way I could have managed moving everything without their help. And they were glad to be able to assist us. It makes others feel good to help. When I look back on it now, that was the last time that group of us was all together. Without Lee, I am not invited to company parties or events. There is no reason for me to get together with his former coworkers. This move was like a small parting, a time of remembrance and saying good-bye, not only to Lee, but to the closeness I shared with them. It was a blessed day in many ways.

Chapter Nine

No Right Way

There is no magic formula or system or checklist for the grieving process. Be warned, I feel there are also no shortcuts. It can be painful and messy and hard, but also beautiful. There will be lots of ups and downs, or two steps forward and one step back! Be patient with yourself.

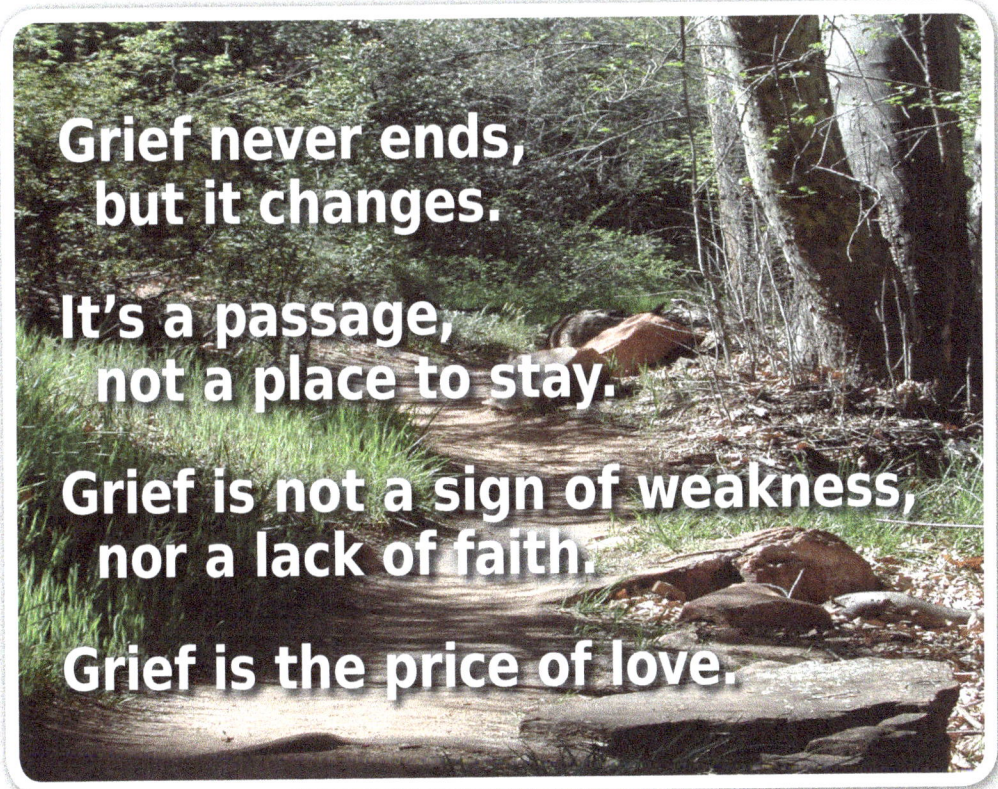

Grief never ends,
  but it changes.

It's a passage,
  not a place to stay.

Grief is not a sign of weakness,
  nor a lack of faith.

Grief is the price of love.

In a Christian devotional, I once read about a woman recently separated from her husband. She wanted to feel better immediately. She wanted to feel better *now*! She didn't want to wait months or years to feel better. You may also feel this way. Remember that healing takes work and energy. You wouldn't go through major surgery and expect to feel better immediately. The physical part of yourself has been through a traumatic event. Naturally, you would give your body rest to heal. Maybe you would seek interventions like physical therapy to get back on your feet. Can you make a connection between physical healing and emotional healing? Can you see that the emotional part of ourselves has been through trauma and that we should give ourselves rest and time and space, and seek help when we need it?

Elizabeth Kubler-Ross said that we need to be strong to handle grief, and that in the process we may discover new strengths we did not realize we had. Although people commented on how strong I was after Lee's death, I didn't want to hear it. I just wanted Lee back! But now, looking back over the years since his death, I think it was certainly true in my case. I found a deeper appreciation for what I did have in my life and an even greater strength in my spiritual beliefs. I wrote songs and poetry during my "dark nights of the soul" that are some of my best work. The grief might slow you down and make you reflect on your own life more. It may cause you to live more in the moment.

Written and compiled by Judith Herr, Hilltop Hospice, Grand Junction, Colorado, the following are messages to yourself that you may adopt to guide your own approach to life from now on:

🙞 *I will not hide my love from others.

🙞 *I resolve to help my friends in need of support.

🙞 *I am strong; I can grow from pain.

🙞 *I intend to live my life to the fullest. My time is precious.

🙞 *I have learned_____.

I mentioned earlier that my mom's death of a heart attack at sixty-one was my first experience with deep grieving. My dad said he found her upstairs in the bathroom when he got home from work. I pressed for more details. He told me that he found her slumped in front of the toilet—panties down. I could only imagine the laugh my mom and her funny, witty aunts had up in heaven about that. "I literally couldn't give a shit anymore!" "Shit happens!" "Life is shit and then you die!" Don't get me wrong: I grieved for my mom. I miss her still. You need to understand that my mom had a great sense of humor, and these funny thoughts would have made her laugh! Thinking of them makes me smile and brings tears to my eyes, which helps me heal.

I wrote the following little essay for our local library's literary magazine, *Messages from the Hidden Lake.* It was published in 2017.

Mojito Madness

My counselor told me, "There's value in purging."

On that night everything in my body was either coming out or up. I swear the crying and puking were so violent it made me wet myself!

I am a responsible "good" girl. I rarely drink. Usually I'm the designated driver, but not the night of my husband's funeral. I had held myself together through sixteen months of torture called liver cancer, leading to the cruelest ending of all, his death.

My vocabulary diminished to one word—"shit." It became my mantra. Everything was "shit." My life—"shit!" My husband's death—"shit!" My in-laws being twenty minutes late to the funeral—"shit!"

So I toast mojitos and myself for getting horribly drunk that night. I purged in a magnificent way, releasing all the shit that life piled on me.

Later my counselor would say, "You know, shit is fertilizer."

On the surface, this may seem an insignificant moment in my life. I'm not proud of it, but I have accepted it. You see, I have been conditioned to do the right thing, even from a young age. I received the "most conscientious" award in fourth grade! After weeks of doing the expected—being the primary caretaker for Lee, taking care of our children, teaching preschool students, attending church—my night of drunkenness and purging was a release. I had held myself together for so long, over days and weeks, that the alcohol helped me let the pain, tension, stress, emotions, anger out. All of it! It gave me the freedom to say it was all "shit!"

This may sound odd, but an hour or so after Lee's death, his sister, Debbie, started telling funny stories about Lee when he was a young boy. A sense of humor can be a blessing in the midst of such pain. Debbie, my children, and I sat around the table alternately laughing and crying. I provided water and tissues for everyone. It's important to drink lots of water, not only because it helps ground the mourner, but also because we need to hydrate after all the tears.

It may sound crass to be laughing right after someone dies, but that laughter serves a purpose. The tears and crying honor the person and are necessary for grieving, but the celebration of that person's life is healing too. It's okay to experience joy in the midst of your pain. Life is messy—like Lee's footprints—and it is not to be taken too seriously. Life is not black and white, all sorrow or all joy. There is a lot of gray, with seemingly opposite feelings blending together. Our laughter and tears, often happening simultaneously, set us on a healthy path towards healing.

Even though I was experiencing anticipatory grief, and I knew Lee was going to die, I was not prepared for his death. I was not prepared for the emotional toll grief would have on me. Even as I write this, eleven years later, the grief comes back in waves. I am surprised by the sobs coming from myself. I've had to put the pen down and be present with the stark, raw pain of loss again.

I was emotionally unprepared for the loss of my husband. I was equally unprepared for the physical death process. Hospice had been involved for about two weeks at the time of Lee's death. His illness progressed very quickly at the end, and I wasn't ready. I had been given some literature from hospice, but put it aside to read later. So I was totally out of my element when Lee began producing a gagging, choking sound. The hospice nurse had just been at our house. My sister-in-law, Debbie, had gone to the nearest town for a few groceries, and our children were at school. My brother-in-law, Ralph, and his wife and infant son were visiting Lee. I started to panic at the horrible noises coming from Lee! I thought maybe he was in pain. Ralph and I tried to mix some pain medication in applesauce, but Lee couldn't eat it. There were suppositories for pain, and we started discussing if that's what was necessary. We really didn't want to go that route (pun intended).

The gasping and choking sounds continued so I called the hospice nurse for advice. She said it sounded like the death gurgle. I exclaimed, "What? What does that mean?" She calmly asked if I had read the literature. I admitted that I hadn't. So she explained that, in her experience, when people are dying they often make a gasping, strangled sound called the "death gurgle." To me the sound was similar to the old coffee pots that used to percolate on the stove. At this point, I was seriously freaking out. Sensing my anxiety, the hospice nurse said she would turn around and come back.

I will never forget that sound, the death gurgle, or how I felt at that moment. I have never felt so helpless or panicked. I was overwhelmed by so many sensations and feelings: nausea, sadness, panic, sadness, fear. My heart was racing frantically. I was in full flight-or-fight mode. I'm sure the time Lee started making the sounds to the time of his last breath was not very long, maybe twenty or thirty minutes. But time stretched and stalled. It seemed like it took forever for the nurse to return.

Lee gasped his last breath that afternoon in November. I screamed "No!" over and over, sobbing uncontrollably. He was already gone. How quickly his physical appearance changed! Seconds after that last breath, his body looked like a shell. The man I loved was gone. He wasn't "here" anymore.

Later I joked to my "safe" people that Lee decided to leave when we were ready to give him the suppository. That's when he said, "That's it! I'm outta here!"

The hospice nurse showed up soon afterward. We dressed Lee in a t-shirt that said, "Silence is golden but duct tape is silver." We sprayed his mouth with peppermint and put some cologne on him before I left to get my children from school.

Driving to the school knowing what I had to tell them, that their dad was dead, is still one of the hardest things I have ever done. I wanted to be the one to tell them, but I dreaded having to give them that news. I cried during the entire twenty-minute drive.

Caleb was young enough that he still believed his dad would get better. He had a big smile on his face as I pulled into the school's parking lot, bless his heart. As he approached the truck and saw the expression on my face, that quickly changed. I told him as gently as I could. He started wailing. Then we had to pick up Brittany, our daughter, at the junior high/high school building five miles away. Being older than Caleb, Brittany had an idea why she was called out of class early. Again, finding the words was a challenge. My heart felt shattered, a thousand shards of glass breaking on the ground. I didn't know if I would ever feel whole again. But somehow, through the blinding tears streaming down my face, I drove us safely back home.

Looking back now after many years, the time seems blurred and distant. I often felt like I was in a fog or a haze. It seemed like time crawled by then. I literally would watch the clock just to get to the next event in the day. Usually we feel there is never enough time in our day. But when you are grieving, the days can seem impossibly long and endless.

Time can become rather arbitrary when we grieve. We long for a way to reverse the flow of days, as Nessa Rapoport does in *A Woman's Book of Grieving*. In "Undo It, Take It Back" she pleads, "Undo it, take it back, make every day the previous one until I am returned to the day before the one that made you gone. Or set me on an airplane traveling west, crossing the date line again and again, losing this day, then that, until the day of loss still lies ahead, and you are here instead of sorrow." As Winnie-the Pooh tells Christopher Robin, "If you live to be a hundred, I want to live to be a hundred minus one day so I never have to live without you."

Another cruel trick of grieving is going to bed and forgetting about our loss while we are asleep. We wake disoriented, and it seems like our loss could have been a dream or a nightmare. Then we remember that our loved one is gone all over again. It takes a moment for our brain to say, "Oh yes, they're not here." This sucks! It only happened to me for a few days, but still. Each time I had that realization it felt like I'd been slapped in the face. It is such a cruel, sickening experience.

Ruth Coughlin, in her book *Grieving: A Love Story,* went straight to my heart. She is a widow, and she's annoyed at everyone else's problems, the everyday, run-of-the mill snafus that dog us on a daily basis. At times, she says, "I would like to tell people that until you experience a loss this big, everything else is amateur night. It is what I have come to call the dwarfing down of reality, the difference between an oak and a bonsai, the unassailable evidence that, compared to death and devastation, the rest of what passes for ordinary life is small change."

I heard my colleagues complaining about their husbands. Their husbands were not helping around the house, their husbands were being stubborn, their husbands were not listening, blah, blah, blah. I wanted to yell (but didn't) that at least they had a husband, even if he was just lying on the couch doing nothing! I wanted to shout, "Go home and hug that lazy so-and-so! Don't wait a minute!" Ruth Coughlin says, "I try not to lash out at my friends and family; I am not that dumb. Without their love, I know that I would be in a padded room somewhere..." I try to follow Coughlin's advice.

Lemony Snicket, author of *A Series of Unfortunate Events,* put it this way in *Horse Radish, Bitter Truths You Can't Avoid:* "Grief, a type of sadness that most often occurs when you have lost someone you love, is a sneaky thing, because it can disappear for a long time, and then pop back up when you least expect it."

Chapter Ten

Gratitude

"We can complain because rose bushes have thorns,
or rejoice because thorns have roses."
Alphonse Karr

Does it seem out of place in a book on grieving to put "Gratitude" for the letter "G?" My rationale is summed up in a French proverb, "Gratitude is the heart's memory."

We will never forget our loss. We will grieve throughout the rest of our lives. Even through the heartache, we can be thankful. Granted, it is not easy sometimes. However, when you realize how your life might have been without your loved one at all, doesn't it make you grateful you had them in your life for the time you did? In Tennyson's poem on the death of his best friend, Arthur Hallam, he wrote, "'tis better to have loved and lost than to never have loved at all." Though the time we had with them may seem too short or not be to our liking, we were better because of them. We are grateful for whatever love they shared, wisdom they imparted, joy they brought. "When eating fruit, remember the one who planted the tree," says a Vietnamese proverb.

I usually have a glass-half-full, optimistic nature. But after my mom died, I had trouble being positive, and negative thoughts were becoming pervasive. Then I began a gratitude journal in which I listed ten things I was grateful for each day. At first the lists were pretty generic, like my family, my health, my job. Gradually the lists changed. They became more about the little wonders I was encountering daily, wonders I had overlooked in my pain and sorrow. I wrote about a preschool student's jokes and the laughter and joy his joking brought me. I noticed the way the breeze ruffled the aspen tree's leaves in my front yard. I marveled at how hard my dog's tail wagged at the sight of my vehicle. As I grew more in tune with my gratitude, my positivity returned. I still use a gratitude journal when I feel the negativity creep back. I strive to be more appreciative by having an "attitude of gratitude."

When our focus is on the good and beautiful, we see more of it in our world. The light of our attention illuminates it. Our appreciation for the beauty and for the positive events in our lives is gratitude that something good exists or has happened. Are you grateful for the memories you have of your loved one? Hold them close to your heart and bless them. Acknowledge your gratitude.

"Gratitude makes sense of our past, brings peace for today, and creates a vision for tomorrow," says Melody Beattie. "It turns denial into acceptance, chaos to order, confusion to clarity." Gratitude helps us see through new eyes and appreciate the goodness around us. Dietrich Bonhoeffer, the courageous anti-Nazi Lutheran pastor, said, "Gratitude changes the pangs of memory into a tranquil joy."

Author and columnist Dan Koeppel wrote a beautiful article entitled "The Afterlife List." His father, an avid birder, had passed and asked Dan to spread his ashes when and where he spots the elusive mountain quail. Dan carried his father's ashes in his car everywhere, hoping for a glimpse of the bird. He had his father's remains with him for so many years that a friend suggested that Dan's father was telling him that he should always be with him. Dan refused to believe that notion and kept believing that someday he would carry out his father's last wish.

After several years, Dan and his five-year-old son finally spotted the mountain quail in Julian, California. Like a tragic comedy, as they released the ashes, a wind whirled the fine powder back into their faces. Concerned for his son's reaction, Dan was surprised to see him smiling. The boy's sweatshirt was caked with the powdered ash, looking like confectioners' sugar. The young boy pressed his hands into the middle of his jacket, leaving a visible handprint.

On the drive home, his son was quiet and thoughtful. He said, "When you're alive, you have your own heart, and that's where you live. But when you die, your heart stops. That means you get to live in the hearts of everybody who was ever your friend and everybody who ever loved you." Dan was speechless at his son's sudden epiphany and the wisdom in his words. His son looked down at his sweatshirt where the handprints were still visible. "You see," he said, "now Grandpa Richard can hug us forever."

"To live in hearts we leave behind is not to die."
—*Thomas Campbell*

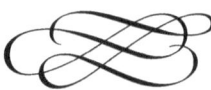

Chapter Eleven

Conclusion

Remember that grief is an affirmation of our love and our ability to care for another. We wouldn't experience loss if we first didn't care. Nessa Rapoport adds, "In the end, the fiercest love cannot avert the hour of dying."

I know I would give all my hard-earned knowledge of grief and the resulting personal growth for one more day with Lee, feelings echoed in the Diamond Rio song "One More Day."

"One more day
One more time
One more sunset, maybe I'd be satisfied
But then again
I know what it would do
Leave me wishing still, for one more day with you."

You may feel, as I do, that we were forced into this situation against our wills. We didn't ask to lose a loved one. We didn't want to learn from pain. Yet here we are. I would give all I have to rewind the past and have Lee here with me again. But we all know how death works, and I will not reject the hard-won knowledge of losing someone I loved so dearly. People told me I was strong, but often I felt weak. Rapoport writes, "When you meet such a woman, do not speak of inner sustenance, of benefit from sorrow or of healing. Nothing but restoration would suffice, and every day the anguish, rather than abating, multiplies. Do not say that time repairs, or talk of moving forward or of growing. Such consolations are absurd. Offer only this: I too, have suffered and endured."

"May the stars carry your sadness away, may the flowers fill your heart
with beauty, may hope forever wipe away your tears, and, above all, may
silence make you strong."
　　　　　　　　　　　　　　　　　　　　　　　　—Chief Dan George

Soon after my husband died, I met my father-in-law outside the mortuary. We talked for a few minutes, and I'll never forget what he said. He called Lee his "hero." This really bothered me because I was certain Lee never knew his father felt that way. My beloved aunt was with me, and I told her about the exchange. She said, "Whatever it takes for him to get back to sleep at 2:00 in the morning, Nene." The point is that we will all etch the memories we want or need. I strive for honesty and truthfulness and not to glamorize the past. Everything I remember is with my own filters though. I wanted to judge my father-in-law for not being truthful. I was angry that he didn't tell Lee that when he was alive. But my aunt's words were wise. He had just lost his son. We must remember in the depths of our own grief, that others are grieving too.

I was crying in the shower one morning after my mom died. My dad had announced he was getting remarried just eight months after her passing. Of course, I wanted what was best for my dad. I was being selfish and childish. I couldn't accept my dad's decision. I told myself it was too soon. I wasn't ready! I did want my dad to be happy though. A true extrovert, my dad was lonely and miserable. My mind was having a terrible time wrapping itself around the idea of a new step-mom. In the midst of this dizzying swirl of emotions, a voice came to me. The voice was crystal clear and firm. It said, "There is room in your heart."

Immediately I felt calmer—and convicted. Of course there was room in my heart. I could accept my dad's new wife into our family and not lose the love I had for my mom. I could be thankful he found someone to be happy with again. I could open my heart.

A few months after the marriage proposal, they separated. But with my dad's next girlfriend, I was able to be at peace with his new relationship and the choices he made in his life.

There is a story about a cracked pitcher that allows more water to flow through it, dribbling water along the path, a path now lined with beautiful flowers watered by the leaky pitcher. Think of your heart like that pitcher. Now that it has been broken and cracked, more love and light will flow through. There is room in your heart too. "The experience of grief is a great gift…for the heart that breaks is just opening again." Sharon Callahan

> "Love lives longer than grief or pain.
> All other things pass,
> But love will remain,
> A bond that nothing can sever
> Because love lasts forever."
> —Jessica St. James

The tenacity and endurance of the ancient juniper trees of the Southwest remind me of the grieving process. It is not easy, but it can lead to blessings if you are willing to do the work.

Following are some suggestions for taking care of yourself, coping, and doing your work while grieving. They are not absolute, nor one-size-fits-all, so please practice them according to your needs.

Breathe.

Our bodies automatically breathe for us, but sometimes we hold our breath. I read about a woman having a painful medical procedure during which the doctor had to stop and tell her to breathe. She didn't even realize she had been holding her breath! When you become stressed, as during a loss, the pain might make you hold your breath. You may tense up and fear letting go. You need to breathe, deeply and fully. Fill your lungs with oxygen and release the carbon dioxide and all the physical and emotional toxins from your body. Repeat many times a day! Take a deep breath and imagine blowing on a dandelion. Or purchase or imagine a pinwheel. Take a deep breath and let it out to blow the pinwheel.

In a January 2014 article in *Prevention* titled "The Healer," Sister Dang Nghiem, MD, says "It's a myth to say that time can heal. Time cannot heal. Breathing and mindfulness can." Sister D lost her partner fourteen years before the article was published. On the morning of her thirty-first birthday, she'd received the devastating phone call that her partner, John, had drowned. Unsure how to move forward after this tremendous loss, she focused on breathing exercises. Being aware of her breathing and practicing deep inhalations and exhalations aided her healing.

One breathing exercise to try is called "square" breathing. Picture the four equal sides of a square in your mind. On the first side of the square, breathe in during four counts. On the second side of the square, hold the breath in for four counts. On the third side of the square, let the breath out during four counts. On the fourth and final side of the square, hold your breath for the four counts.

Meditate/Pray.

Many meditation apps and programs are available. Find one that works for you. Meditation is simply quieting the mind. It will bring more peace and tranquility into your life. Meditation can relieve stress, clear your head, and strengthen your immune system. Find a comfortable position for your body and breathe in and out. Let your thoughts pass through your mind without judgement, but don't become stuck in them. Return to focusing on your breathing and come back to a blank mind. You may want to repeat a word like "om" or "peace" or any phrase that resonates with you. For example, you might breathe in on the word "sorrow" and exhale on the word "healing." (Let sorrow be replaced by healing.)

If you are someone who can't sit still, you might try yoga "movement meditation." You will find articles and lessons on this kind of meditation on the Internet, or there may be a local yoga instructor who can help you.

You will find scripture and prayers in the appendix for you to consider. Prayer is our connection to God or our higher power.

Move.

Our human bodies are designed for movement, not sitting all day. Take a walk. Exercise. Do yoga or stretch. Go to a gym. Play a sport. Moving helps with depression and is essential to functioning productively.

Create a routine or ritual.

Routines can soothe us. Their repetition is calming. After the death of my husband, I created my own morning ritual. I would wake up, make a cup of tea, and listen to Five for Fighting's song "100 Years." I usually cried while I sipped my tea, cried in the shower, and sometimes I cried as I put on my makeup for the day. Near the end of Lee's illness, he stroked my cheeks one time and said I had on my war paint. Sometimes I felt I had to put on a different face for the world. So "war paint" seemed accurate to what I was experiencing at the time.

Five for Fighting wasn't Lee's favorite band, and not one of the songs on the album was "our song." But somehow the lyrics spoke to me at that time. My morning routine anchored me for the coming day. By being with my emotions for that brief, precious time every morning, I felt better prepared to face the rest of the day.

Rituals can become sacred events. They give us space and time to spiritually express ourselves. They elevate the ordinary into the holy, like my counselor's Holy Days gatherings.

Focus.

Become mindful. Be fully present in the moment. Pay attention to yourself, to your five senses. Be surprised by what you see, hear, feel, and smell. Eat a meal mindfully, focusing on one bite of food at a time. Pay attention to little wonders. Swirl a snow globe and notice the drifting white snowflakes. Watch a sprinkler or fountain spray water. Notice birds outside your window. Reflect on the cycles of nature. Pause to observe your surroundings. Hone in on what matters, the essentials of your existence. Allow for your perspectives to change: consider your options. As Benjamin Franklin said, "Chase butterflies and they will never be caught; watch butterflies and they will come to you."

Or don't focus/Be mindless.

Let your lens get hazy and unfocused. Drift in a stream of consciousness where the destination is unknown. As Osho says, "In the space of no-mind, truth descends like light."

Be gracious and grateful.

Express your gratitude. Thank others. Thank your family and friends. Thank the people who give you support. Thank your departed loved one. Thank God or whatever higher power gives you strength.

Being gracious and kind can change our brain, improve our immune system, help with depression, and improve our relationships.

Count the blessings you have. Focus on the positives you still have when you feel discouraged.

"When you arise in the morning, give thanks for the morning light, for your life and strength. Give thanks for your food and the joy of living. If you see no reason for giving thanks, the fault lies in yourself."
—Chief Tecumseh

A Prayer:

Our Most Loving God,

We are thankful to have had our loved one here on earth. They were our companion, walking with us through this world to know and to love. Console us when we mourn. Grant us faith to see that in death lies the path to eternal life. Remind us to walk in your ways with strength and grace until we are reunited with You, Christ Jesus, and those that have gone before us. Amen

"If the only prayer you ever say in your entire life is thank you, it will be enough."

Meister Eckhart

Feel.

Give yourself permission to experience a full range of emotions. Do not bottle them up or hide them. Remember that feelings are not right or wrong, they just are. They change. Allow them to come and then release them.

Challenge yourself.

Set a personal goal and work to achieve it. Write, sing, draw, run a 5K, or create a charity. As Morgan Freeman once said, "Challenge yourself: It's the only path which leads to growth."

Plan something to look forward to.

Sister Dang Nghiem in the aforementioned *Prevention* article talks about planning positive outcomes for the future, to cultivate joy and peace, even though you may still feel pain. "It's like a garden: You have to take care of the weeds, but you also have to plant flowers. If you only weed, you'll be exhausted and lose hope. And if you plant enough flowers, eventually there will be less room for all the weeds."

Plant some "seeds" for you to later enjoy in your "garden." When I was going through Lee's clothes, I saved many of them. I knew I wanted to have quilts made out of them for each of my children at their high school graduation.

I believe we yearn to feel vibrantly alive after being surrounded by death. I needed to have some things to look forward to. That adrenaline rush of getting a tattoo or climbing Mt. Blanca felt good after feeling numb. However, I think that the numbness has its place too. It can be our defense when the emotions of the grieving process are too much to bear. But I would not want any of us to stay there. Humans want to move forward. As one of my dearest friends says, "Even if I fall on my face, at least I'm moving forward!"

I ordered unicorn checks after my husband's death. I have loved unicorns since I was girl, and back then they were rare. This may seem insignificant, but Lee and I had a joint banking account, and he never would have agreed to unicorns! So, knowing that now I was solely in charge of the finances for our family was a burden. The unicorn checks I would write were a little bright spot in the midst of this heavy responsibility.

Plan something special on your birthday. Enroll in a class. Join a choir. Play a game with friends. Host a game night. Go to a movie. Cook your favorite food. Plant a garden or some flowers. Give yourself something to look forward to.

Tell your story.

Every time you tell your story, there is healing. You stop your body's stress responses and activate relaxation response that release healing hormones like dopamine and endorphins. Brene Brown says, "Owning our story and loving ourselves through that process is the bravest thing we will ever do." Just choose your confidants carefully and use them. Be truthful with your feelings and share with these "safe" people. Trying to protect others is not honoring them and their truth. Silence is not always golden. Kim McManus reminds us, "Your heartache is someone else's hope. If you make it through, somebody else is going to make it through. Tell your story."

Learn something new.

Be willing to change. Cook a new dish. Enroll in a class. Read a novel or a how-to on a topic unfamiliar to you. Learn a new language. Try a new activity, hobby or sport.

Do something meaningful.

Do work that feels purposeful to you. Stay busy, but avoid frantic activity that could be detrimental to healing.

Live your life intentionally, in the present moment. Try not to dwell on the future or the past. In the book *Turn Around Bright Eyes: The Rituals of Love and Karaoke*, Rob Sheffield discovers that singing karaoke is therapeutic for him after the loss of his girlfriend. He uses the music to express his emotions, and the lyrics speak of his pain and loss. He also learns to live in the moment and not dwell on the past. He says, "Trying to live in the past didn't work for me, and it's only now that I fully realize I'm incredibly lucky it didn't. Because it would have been all too sad to miss out on right now. That would have turned the past into a fraud. It would have meant all my happy memories were a lie. It would have meant all that time and all that love was a waste, leading up to a wasted future…It's scary to think of how I could have gotten stuck pining for the past."

There is a Quaker saying "proceed as way opens." This means being open to opportunities and living in the present moment to accept them, going with the flow of your being right now, proceeding as you learn new ways of being.

Thomas Moore in *Dark Nights of the Soul,* encourages us to be "more" of who we are. He says, "It is never easy to accept more life, never easy to become more of who you are. It is challenging in the extreme to really live life instead of taking it in portions that are comfortable or convenient for you." Your loss already is challenging you, maybe in ways you never expected.

Help others.

Kind actions matter. In the Buddhist tradition, karma means actions, thoughts, and speech. Although it may not seem much to open the door for a stranger, to smile at someone, or to return the coin dropped by the person in line ahead of you, it does. Everything we do can be a more thoughtful choice. In helping others, we can help ourselves.

Volunteering may be the purposeful work you need. It may help you to feel needed and valued and give you a sense of community. Share your talents and skills with others.

Take a vacation.

Get away from your usual place and pace. Go for a drive somewhere you've never been. Enjoy a cuisine you've never tried before. Visit a museum or art gallery in a different city. Refresh your vision by changing your geography, however briefly.

Rest.

Grief can be an exhausting process. Take naps. Get a massage. See an acupuncturist. Read. Slow down. Watch a sunset or go star-gazing. Renew.

Find Meaning.

I will caution you on finding meaning. When I was getting my Master's degree in counseling, we discussed the meaning of some of life's biggest challenges. My cohorts and I batted around lessons we had learned in our own lives. We agreed that in those dark moments, we felt awful. But what was the reward for the pain? Did everything in life have a purpose? One of my favorite professors, Dr. Varhely, blew my mind when she said, "Maybe the lesson was to know what it felt like to feel like shit!" Be aware that this is possible.

In *A Woman's Book of Grieving* Nessa Rapoport posits the possible meaning of suffering: "This is the teaching of suffering…Like a dancer who offers years of bloodied feet and tender injury toward a gift, a moment of perfect, elusive grace, we proceed through our buffeted lives, trying to make of ill fortune and random blows one small and beautiful thing, which all of us deserve, not because of talent or means but simply because we live."

Steadfast Hope

Out of times of tremendous trial
sprout seasons of abundant growth.

> Joan Marie Arbogast,
> *children's book author and freelance writer*

You may have asked why, shouted, "Why!" You may have shaken your fists at God or the sky, or knelt and whispered "Why?" The word becomes a mantra for many of us who are grieving. You have probably realized that there really is no acceptable answer. If you are part of a faith community, others may help comfort you or aid you in finding some answers through faith or a spiritual connection.

Last Word

My sister died suddenly at the age twenty-one,
and no one was ready.
The whys were unanswered,
the sorrow immense.
But God sent people—
strangers who read of the accident
wrote and prayed,
friends faced their fears of not saying the right words,
and came.

Then God spoke comfort
through Scripture,
Bearing witness that all the brokenness
we bring and yield in Jesus' name
is gathered up, redeemed,
and given back as peace.

And God spoke hope
in the overcoming act of Resurrection,
that death is not the end,
that beyond our sight and understanding,
the final word
is joy.

> Roberta Porter

Roberta Porter lost her sister in a midair plane collision in December of 1960. Her sister had been working as a flight attendant for less than a year.

Debra Jarvis is a hospital chaplain, writer, and host of the podcast "The Art of Risk." In her article, "Down Off the Cross," in the October 2016 *Reader's Digest*, she identifies how claiming our experience and finding meaning in it is essential to coping with it. "We know that the way to cope with trauma, loss, or any other life-changing experience is to find meaning. But here's the thing: No one can tell us what that meaning is. We have to decide what it means. And that meaning can be quiet and private—we don't need to start a foundation, write a book, or work on a documentary. Instead, perhaps we make one small decision about our lives that can bring about big change." Viktor Frankl echoes her words, "Life is never made unbearable by circumstances, but only by lack of meaning and purpose."

As a hospital chaplain, Jarvis goes on to tell the story of a cancer patient who was under her care. She noticed that this young man was alone. He lived by himself, always came into chemotherapy alone, and left the hospital without anyone accompanying him. Yet she was aware that he had a lot of friends on the infusion floor. In fact, the staff thought so much of him that at his last chemo treatment, they had a celebration for him. Jarvis asked him, "What are you going to do now?" He answered, "Make friends." He began volunteer work and attending church. Jarvis was later invited to his home for a Christmas party. It was filled with many of his new friends. This young man, she concludes, "decided that the meaning of his experience was to know the joy of friendship, and he learned to make friends."

Be patient with yourself.

Roll with the tides of your grief. Accept the highs and the lows. Grief is often a rollercoaster of emotions by nature. You may backslide after feeling relatively good and plunge back into your sadness, despair, or anger. This may happen many times. Give yourself permission to do it. Remember that we are all human. We are not made to stay in this hyper-stressful state. "Backsliding" lets us experience these intense emotions more gradually, a little at a time.

Mother Teresa said, "I know God will not give me anything I can't handle. I just wish that He didn't trust me so much." When my son, Caleb, read this in one of our church's bulletins, he sighed, "I know exactly what that means."

In *The Gift of an Ordinary Day*, Katrina Kenison speaks of the heaviness of loss and acknowledges that the burden will always be with us. This is why we need to be patient with ourselves. She continues, though, that with every ending there is a beginning: "I allow, just for a moment, the past to push hard against the walls of my heart. Being alive, it seems, means learning to bear the weight of the passing of all things. It means finding a way to lightly hold all the places we've loved and left anyway…it means, always, allowing for the hard truth of endings. It means, too, keeping faith in beginnings."

How do you know when you're feeling better?

Although there is no timeline for the grieving process, there will be a time when you feel different. Your sense of humor will return. You may be able to laugh at the absurdities of living. Your mood swings will not be as vast, the highs and lows not as disparate. There will be longer spans of time between upsets.

You may be able to see blessings or some positive affirmations from your loss. You may find you are able to live with the seeming opposites of sorrow and happiness. In my life, I made a distinction between contentedness and happiness. I strive to be content. Being happy is great, but I know that it can be temporary. Nessa Rapaport puts it this way: "It is the hardest of all learning that the opposite of depression is not happiness—a radiant, receding goal—but vitality, to feel alive each minute you are given. Then when sweetness comes it is most sweet and when sorrow comes you know its name. In the aftermath of suffering, you chart each day as an explorer preceding map or compass, and what you find is shockingly alloyed. All happiness is dappled, and even bleakest tragedy has moments of strange praise."

As you progress in your healing, you may be able to give more human qualities to your deceased loved one. You may be able to see their weaknesses as well as the pedestal you put them on. You may be able to admit to the imperfections in your relationship, as good as it may have been.

"You may not control all the events that happen to you, but you can decide not to be reduced by them," said Maya Angelou. Your life is in your hands and you are capable of taking charge of it. You may find that you can make responsible decisions in determining your quality of life.

Katrina Kenison found solace in "letting go…not just an idea or a gesture, but a kind of spiritual maturation, a movement away from the physical realm into a place of greater faith and mystery…reinvention seems always to require some painful elements of rejection and tearing down. But as we change, so do all things change. To hold on tight is to miss out on opportunities for growth and movement. Letting go, stepping forward into the unknown, we discover our capacities for resilience and faith, and we begin to glimpse our unique potential, to realize it in ways we couldn't have begun to imagine just a short time ago."

When you realize that you are resilient and capable, that you are still growing, learning and loving, you are most likely doing "better."

When to Seek Professional Help.

If grief becomes an ongoing presence in your life, taking over your thoughts and becoming a primary focus in your daily events, this becomes complicated grief, traumatic grief, or prolonged grief. The process of recovery or healing is stopped. You are stuck and cannot return to the "new normal" of life. Although hard to define, if you have difficulty moving on and bitterness and anger over the loss persists for longer than six months, it may be complicated grief. If you have the following symptoms, listed in "Gradients of Grief: Understanding the Different Forms of Grief" by Kat Smith September 12, 2019 https://blog.memd.me/signs-of-complicated-grief/, then yours could be complicated grief:

- Anger and frequent mood swings

- Lethargy and overall lack of energy

- Reluctance to return to work and normal routines

- Obsession with a deceased loved one, such as refusal to donate the individual's old clothing or alter his or her bedroom

- Aversion to reminders of the loved one and refusal to talk about the individual in conversation

- Ongoing issues keeping up with work or school

- Intense feelings of sadness, bitterness, or longing

- Substance abuse and self-destructive behaviors

- Thoughts of suicide

- Decreased attention to personal grooming and appearance

- Aggravated symptoms of existing mental health conditions, such as depression or anxiety disorder

If you are experiencing complicated grief, you may need to work with a behavioral health specialist to overcome it. Please seek help if this is the case for you.

I still find comfort in remembering the love of my mom and my husband. "Death may take a person from out of your future, but it cannot remove the loved one from your past. Even when you have lost someone you love, you have not lost the love," says Harold S. Kusher. The following poem from a sympathy card I received expresses the same idea:

"Death leaves a heartache
No one can heal.
Love leaves a memory
No one can steal."

I know it can be hard to hear that you are strong, and you may not feel that way right now, but there is courage in muddling our way through this process.

"Strength doesn't come from what you can do. It comes from overcoming the things you once thought you couldn't."

Rikki Rogers

I believe in you. I am proud of you, and you should be proud of yourself. Your life has changed dramatically and permanently. You are choosing the path to healing. I hope you continue growing, learning, and loving. "Promise me you'll always remember: You're braver than you believe, and stronger than you seem, and smarter than you think." —Christopher Robin to Winnie-the Pooh

In her novel *Church of the Dog* Kaya McLauren writes, "…the Grand Canyon… is like a giant wound formed from the natural cycles of life, and what I find comforting about being here is people's acceptance of it. No one sits here and tells the Earth that time will heal this wound, and no one calls the processes that created it 'tragic.' No one expects the Earth here to be like it was before the river cut the canyon. People leave it alone and find beauty in it as it is."

The most beautiful people
we have known are those
who have known defeat,
known suffering,
known struggle,
known loss,
and have found their way
out of the depths.

These persons have an appreciation,
a sensitivity,
and an understanding of life
That fills them with compassion,
gentleness, and a deep loving concern.

Beautiful people don't just happen.

The Voice of La Puente Winter 2018

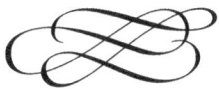

Appendix

Christian Prayers and Scriptures for Comfort and Healing

Lamentations 3:22-26; 31-33 (New Revised Standard Version)

22 *The steadfast love of the Lord never ceases,*
      his mercies never come to an end;

23 *they are new every morning;*
      great is your faithfulness.

24 *"The Lord is my portion," says my soul,*
      "therefore I will hope in him."

25 *The Lord is good to those who wait for him,*
      to the soul that seeks him.

26 *It is good that one should wait quietly*
      for the salvation of the Lord.

31 *For the Lord will not*
      reject forever.

32 *Although he causes grief, he will have compassion*
      according to the abundance of his steadfast love;

33 *for he does not willingly afflict*
      or grieve anyone.

Psalm 23 –King James Version

The Lord is my shepherd; I shall not want.

He maketh me to lie down in green pastures: he leadeth me beside the still waters.

He restoreth my soul: he leadeth me in the paths of righteousness for his name's sake.

Yea, though I walk through the valley of the shadow of death, I will fear no evil: for thou art with me; thy rod and thy staff they comfort me.

Thou preparest a table before me in the presence of mine enemies: thou anointest my head with oil; my cup runneth over.

Surely goodness and mercy shall follow me all the days of my life: and I will dwell in the house of the Lord for ever.

I Thessalonians 4:13:

Because God is with me, even in grief I can have hope.

John 14:27

Peace I leave with you; My peace I give to you; not as the world gives, do I give to you. Let not your heart be troubled, nor let it be fearful."

Psalm 18:28

For Thou dost light my lamp; The Lord my God illumines my darkness.

Psalm 71:5

For thou art my hope; O Lord God, Thou art my confidence from my youth.

Psalm 73:26

My flesh and my heart may fail, but God is the strength of my heart and my portion forever.

Episcopal Prayer:

The very love we have for each other in Christ brings deep sorrow when we are parted by death. Jesus himself wept at the grave of his friend. So, while we rejoice that one we love has entered into the nearer presence of the Lord, we sorrow in sympathy with those who mourn."

The Serenity Prayer

God, grant me the serenity
to accept the things I cannot change,
the courage to change the things I can,
and the wisdom to know the difference.

"For Those Who Mourn"

Gracious God,
as your Son wept with Mary and Martha at the tomb of Lazarus, look
with compassion on those who grieve, especially (Name of person)
Grant them the assurance of your presence now
and faith in your eternal goodness,
that in them may be fulfilled the promise
that those who mourn shall be comforted;
through Jesus Christ our Lord. Amen

From The United Methodist Hymnal, page 461

On the Death of the Beloved

Though we need to weep your loss,
You dwell in that safe place in our hearts
Where no storm or night or pain can reach you.

Your love was like the dawn
Brightening over our lives,
Awakening beneath the dark
A further adventure of color.

The sound of your voice
Found for us
A new music
That brightened everything.

Whatever you enfolded in your gaze
Quickened in the joy of its being;
You placed smiles like flowers
On the altar of the heart.
Your mind always sparkled
With wonder at things.

Though your days here were brief,
Your spirit was alive, awake, complete.

We look toward each other no longer
From the old distance of our names;
Now you dwell inside the rhythm of breath,
As close to us as we are to ourselves.

Though we cannot see you with outward eyes,
We know our soul's gaze is upon your face,
Smiling back at us from within everything
To which we bring our best refinement.

Let us not look for you only in memory,
Where we would grow lonely without you.
You would want us to find you in presence,
Beside us when beauty brightens,
When kindness glows
And music echoes eternal tones.

When orchids brighten the earth,
Darkest winter has turned to spring;
May this dark grief flower with hope
In every heart that loves.

May you continue to inspire us:
To enter each day with a generous heart.
To serve the call of courage and love
Until we see your beautiful face again
In that land where there is no more separation,
Where all tears will be wiped from our mind,
And where we will never lose you again.

John O'Donahue

Do Not Stand at My Grave and Weep

Do not stand at my grave and weep
I am not there. I do not sleep.
I am a thousand winds that blow.
I am the diamond glints on snow.
I am the sunlight on ripened grain.
I am the gentle autumn rain.
When you awaken in the morning's hush
I am the swift uplifting rush
Of quiet birds in circled flight.
I am the soft stars that shine at night.
Do not stand at my grave and cry:
I am not there. I did not die.

Attributed to Mary Elizabeth Frye

On Eagle's Wings

"And God will raise you up on eagle's wings,
Bear you on the breath of dawn,
Make you to shine like the sun,
And hold you in the palm of God's hand."

Michael Joncas United Methodist Hymnal No. 143

Let It Be *(Excerpt)*

When I find myself in times of trouble
Mother Mary comes to me
Speaking words of wisdom
Let it be...
Let it be, let it be, let it be, yeah, let it be
There will be an answer
Let it be
Let it be"

Paul McCartney

*"Seashells remind us that every passing life
leaves something beautiful behind."*

(Sympathy card)

About the Author

Jenene Holcomb is a widow with two grown children. She holds a B.A. in elementary education with a minor in vocal music, as well as an M.A. in counseling. Currently the director, teacher, and Colorado Preschool Program coordinator for her rural school district in southern Colorado, Jenene has taught for twenty-six years. She enjoys tennis, pickleball, and participating in community choir and theater productions. Future plans? More international adventures with her amazing friend and best travel partner, Ty!

Suggested Reading/Bibliography

Coughlin, Ruth. *Grieving: A Love Story,* Independently published, February 9, 2017

Dennison, Amy and Allie & Dave Dennison. *After You Lose Someone You Love: Advice and Insight from the Diaries of Three Kids Who've Been There,* Free Spirit Publishing, Inc., October 1, 2010

Ephron, Delia. *Sister Mother Husband Dog,* Plume; Reprint edition, August 26, 2014

Gilbert, Allison. *Passed and Present: Keeping Memories of Loved Ones Alive,* Seal Press; Illustrated edition, April 12, 2016

Kenison, Katrina. *The Gift of an Ordinary Day: A Mother's Memoir,* Grand Central Publishing, August 20, 2009

Kubler-Ross, Elizabeth, and David Kessler. *On Grief and Grieving: Finding the Meaning of Grief Through the Five Stages of Loss,* Scribner; 1st edition, August 1, 2014

Levine, Arlene Gay. *39 Ways to Open Your Heart,* Conari Press, April 1, 1996. See www.arlenegaylevine.com for a changing sampling of Levine's poems. (Last accessed January 25, 2022)

Levine, Arlene Gay. "For a Dear One at a Dark Time." Unable to determine source.

O'Donohue, John. (1956-2008) *To Bless the Space Between Us,* Convergent Books, March 4, 2008

Rapoport, Nessa. *A Woman's Book of Grieving,* W. Morrow; 1st edition, January 1, 1994

Richo, David. *The Five Things We Cannot Change…and the Happiness We Find by Embracing Them,* Shambhala; Reprint edition, June 13, 2006

Smith, Kat. *Gradients of Grief: Understanding the Different Forms of Grief,* https://blog.memd.me/?s=gradients+of+grief, September 12, 2019

Wallace, Tracey. "Death Rituals, Ceremonies, & Traditions Around the World," https://eterneva.com/blog/death-rituals/ (Last accessed January 25, 2022)

https://whatsyourgrief.com/ A website for grief support.
(Last accessed January 25, 2022)

www.ingramcontent.com/pod-product-compliance
Lightning Source LLC
Chambersburg PA
CBHW041517120626
46551CB00018B/2466